OAK ISLAND, KNIGHTS TEMPLAR, AND THE HOLY GRAIL

Oak Island, Knights Templar, and the Holy Grail:

Secrets of "The Underground Project" REVEALED

Scott F. Wolter & Donald A. Ruh

North Star Press of St. Cloud
www.NorthStarPress.com
Since 1969

Print ISBN: 978-1-68201-152-2
Ebook ISBN: 978-1-68201-153-9

Printed in the United States of America

First Edition

North Star Press of St. Cloud Inc.
www.northstarpress.com

Titles set in Nelson Engraved and Mason Serif OT. Text body set in Minion Pro.

DEDICATIONS:

To my kids, Grant and Amanda,
and to my grandchildren....
-Scott

To Phillip and Caryl LaBarbera and James and
Frank Leone. Some of my oldest and dearest
friends.
-Don

CONTENTS

Foreword:

Janet Wolter

The rumors are true. The medieval Knights Templar did come west to the new world and buried their treasures, yes plural... not just the one on Oak Island but many in different places around the northeast coast of North America. Their motive? To escape the continuous persecution of the Roman Catholic Church and the feudalistic system's control over individuals, by founding their own Free Templar State. That's a bold statement to be sure, but the evidence trail is solid.

It was about 24 years ago that Scott Wolter and I first learned about a beautifully carved rune stone found in 1898 here in our home state of Minnesota, when it was brought into his forensic lab to be examined. It's known as the Kensington Rune Stone, named after the town near where it was found by a farmer clearing trees on his land, and for the Scandinavian runic characters expertly carved in 9 rows on its face and 3 more rows on its cleaved side. The stone is roughly tombstone-shaped and was found wrapped tightly in the roots of a tree. The Swedish immigrant farmer discoverer, Olof Ohman, was familiar with runes from his homeland, but he could not read them because it was a very old alphabet. But his discovery of the stone caused a heated debate that continues to this day.

If you're wondering what this stone has to do with the Oak Island treasure mystery, the answer is everything! For Scott and I, this controversial artifact is what launched us into our study and research regarding pre-Columbian visitors to North America—a controversy because scholars did not accept that any Europeans had arrived before Columbus, except for the Vikings in the far northern Canadian maritime islands and coastal region. The Kensington stone is self-dated by the carver to 1362—Medieval times in

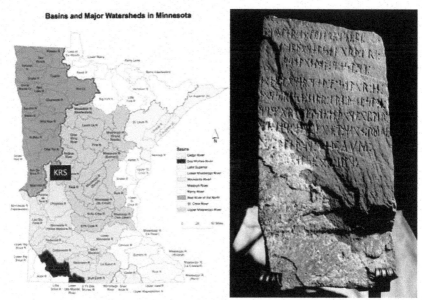

This watersheds map of Minnesota (left) shows where the Kensington Rune Stone (right) was found along the Red River-Mississippi River watershed divide. (Internet)

Europe, and several decades after the Knights Templar were arrested by the king of France and the Pope in 1307.

Many historians believe that was the end of the Templar Order, but through our studies and research we came to know that the Templars didn't disappear into history but went underground, changed the name of the Order, and hid in countries whose monarchs aligned with them. They went on to become part of the story of Oak Island and beyond, but more importantly to change the course of history as one of the most important "influencer" organizations of the last 1,000 years.

The Kensington stone proved to be a Templar document carved in stone, a combination of ritual allegory and the reality of their journey.

But why would they leave Europe and travel "far to the west" all the way to North America and follow the St. Lawrence River into the Great Lakes to the headwaters in the center of the continent in what is now Minnesota? We theorize they did it because it was a known land claim practice among Europeans to place a carved stone or plaque at the headwaters of a watershed, allowing the first to reach it to claim the waterway and all the associated land it drained. Minnesota has three headwaters within the state, the Red River of the North to Hudson Bay, the Mississippi River, and the St. Louis River and Great Lakes—that's the equivalent of claiming half the continent!

The Kensington Rune stone became the center of heated controversy during farmer Ohman's lifetime and beyond. He was mercilessly accused of having carved it, being a Scandinavian himself. But it was not a 19th century hoax as scholars of the era concluded, which was proved by Scott's modern day geologic study of the weathering of the carved characters proving they were at least 200 years old or more at the time of the discovery in 1898. There were no Europeans settlers here in Minnesota in the 17th century, therefore no hoaxers. Scott, a licensed professional geologist, properly used the Scientific Method as any qualified scientist always does: hard science procedures and provable conclusions that can be repeated by other geologists who one day may wish to put the Kensington stone inscription through testing again.

Scott was also able to determine the Kensington stone's mineral composition which proved it was native to Minnesota, not a stone carved in Scandinavia and brought here by 19th century immigrants. The stone was found, expertly dressed to the desired size, the message carved in Scandinavian runes, and then buried as a land claim. Based on the message—the allegory, symbolism, and numerology within it, we determined the party of 30 men it described were in fact, Templar Knights, who left Europe in 1358 and left the stone as a record in 1362. They made no land claim for a specific monarch, and since the Templars were free to move about from country to country, this made perfect sense.

The reader will learn within the pages of this book what their true motive and mission was: to found and form their "New Atlantis," a place of freedom and independence, rights to practice any form of faith, where rights of the individual were Deity given, not by a reigning monarch. Sound familiar? The United States of America was ultimately the result of what we have learned was the true mission of the Knight Templar: bring their wealth in the form of treasure to their sanctuary in the west and found their Free Templar State.

The treasure buried on Oak Island was just one of many caches they left. They bonded with the indigenous peoples, whom they had similar ideology with regarding the duality of the masculine and feminine aspects of Deity, who guarded their treasure sites while they were away.

Scott will also point out to you that there exists other evidence such as the Narragansett Rune Stone and the nearby Newport Tower and other artifacts and sites that prove it was our brethren, the brave Knights Templar, who came here to keep their vast wealth safe. It would ultimately be used

The mysterious stone and mortar structure called Newport Tower, stands in Newport, Rhode Island, and its origin has been the subject of debate since the late 18th Century. The evidence presented in this book provides conclusive evidence it is a medieval astronomical observatory built by the fugitive Knights Templar order. (Wolter/2024)

to fight for and found their "Free Templar State"—what later came to be called, by their Freemason brothers and Founding Father descendants who completed the mission, the United States of America.

As I wrap up my Foreword, I also want to tell the reader you will enjoy the commentary by our good friend, Don Ruh, a cantankerous but soft-hearted 81-year-old man, who has had an amazing life, which you will read about. I have fond memories of our treasure-hunting adventures with Don, where we have come to know him from many walks in the woods and talks over evening meals, about his many life experiences. We also made quite a few more of our own with him: from getting soaked in downpours, to climbing mountains, exploring caves, fording creeks (not always successfully staying dry), tracking him in dense forest when he got separated from us (we were the ones who got lost, of course), metal detecting, and finding old coins, but mostly just being outdoors and enjoying the adventures. Our story is far from over, for I hope there are many more amazing adventures to come.

DAVID S. BRODY

I was part of the original group that climbed Hunter Mountain in 2009 with Don Ruh, Steve St. Clair, Scott Wolter, and Scott's son, Grant. At the time, I believed the collection of documents we now call the Cremona Document to be a confounding mystery, full of both promise and peril. On the one hand, the story the documents told, and the level of detail in which they told it, had the ability to rewrite the history of North America. This was truly an amazing saga—a Templar mission to North America in the late 1100s, involving both treasure and tribulation. On the other hand, the lawyer in me was immediately wary. We found a remarkable artifact (known as the "In Camera Stone"), then a short time later found yet another carved stone (the "Dove Stone"). Were we that good at sleuthing, or were we being played?

Fifteen years later, I still don't know the answer.

In his introductory comments to this book, Scott lists a number of what he calls "yellow flags." It is hard to get past these, especially in light of what we know about Don. Don spent a career in counterintelligence and reportedly is adept at code-making and document forgery. He has admitted to fabricating at least two artifacts relevant to this mystery. Likewise, Diana Muir (who claims to have found the Weems journals, which seem to corroborate some of the material in the Cremona Document) has a past that, according to newspaper accounts, includes admitting to the FBI that she was part of a haox involving non-existent letters from Church of the Latter-Day Saints founders, Joseph Smith and Brigham Young. In examining historical documents and artifacts, provenance is crucial. Frankly, it is difficult to imagine a scenario where provenance is more in question than with the Cremona Document and the Weems journals.

In light of the above, why—a decade and a half later—am I still willing to expend time and energy on this mystery? Because, at least with the Cremona Document, it just doesn't make sense to me as a fake. What is the motivation? Where is the payoff? How could it have been accomplished? None of these questions can easily be answered. Here's what I mean:

In my experience, most hoaxes are perpetrated for some kind of gain, usually financial. As far as I can determine, Don has sold a few hundred copies of his book, *The Scrolls of Onteora* (his Amazon ranking at the time of this writing is 1,250,545[th]), received a few hundred dollars as reimbursement for out-of-pocket expenses, and, well, that's it. If this is a fake, he's been working on it for the better part of two decades, producing hundreds of pages of text along with dozens of maps, codes, drawings, artifacts and aliases. Why? Who would devote so much time and effort to such a fruitless endeavor? One could argue that perhaps Don is looking for attention. If so, again, the returns have been meager. He has not made any television appearances and, as far as I know, has only been featured in a handful of other media events. If this was a hoax perpetuated by Donald Ruh for profit or publicity, well, the joke is on him.

It also would be surprising for someone to perpetuate a hoax which caused that same person damage or harm. By all accounts, Don is an observant and devout Christian. In his book, he concludes on page 369 by listing a series of teachings of Jesus, then writes, "Though we have not learned to do these, we may yet learn by the grace of God and my Lord Jesus Christ." Yet, as you will read in a subsequent book to be released by Scott in the near future, one of the revelations in the Cremona Document is that the skull of Jesus may be buried here in America. According to Christian dogma, the skull of Jesus, of course, has ascended to heaven. Why would a devout Christian propagate a hoax which calls into question something so fundamental to his own faith? It simply does not make sense.

I also find it difficult to believe that Don would have had the knowledge needed to orchestrate a fraud of this magnitude. Whoever wrote the Cremona Document (whether real or fake) exhibited a vast knowledge of both Templar history and Freemasonry. No doubt, Don is a highly intelligent and capable individual. But he is not a trained historian, and I don't believe he is a Freemason. I supposed it is possible he had assistance from a Freemasonic friend or associate, but it would be an extraordinary and rare thing for a Masonic brother to assist in a fraud of this nature and magnitude.

Finally, as you read through this, you will see descriptions of events which, to my eye, would seem impossible for one person to fabricate. In some cases, the events are too complex or elaborate, in some they require too much hidden knowledge, and in some they are based on information unknown at the time the events occurred. Don is a man of limited means. In addition to my training as an attorney, I have written 21 thriller/mystery novels. I understand evidence and also complex plotting. Based on my training and experience, I believe a hoax of this magnitude would require resources and assets beyond those Don has had access to.

I recognize that it is odd, and less than ideal, to release a book in which there are still so many questions about the validity of key material and disclosures within it. But this is one of those stories that keeps evolving. Every year, it seems, new material comes to light (yes, I recognize that this, too, could be considered a "yellow flag"). If we wait for full and perfect knowledge, the book might never be written. The advantages of publishing now are twofold, I believe. First, doing so establishes a written record. Don is 81 years old. Scott and Janet both have many other projects they are working on. In life, the unexpected can happen. If the book isn't published now, it might never be. This is an incredibly detailed and complex story. We need a written record for posterity, even if that record is an imperfect one. Second, by putting this information out to the public, other researchers will be able to analyze, critique, evaluate and weigh in on the mystery. A simple example will illustrate my point. As Scott writes in his foreword, there are questions as to whether William Jackson is a real person. Perhaps someone will read this book and recognize Jackson as a former neighbor, classmate, or colleague, thereby answering that open question.

I want to conclude by offering a public thanks to Scott and Janet. They have been doggedly chasing this mystery for 15 years, expending vast amounts of time, money, and energy. They have also been, and no doubt will continue to be, the target of public ridicule. However, were it not for them, it is likely this story would never have been told. As I wrote above, I recognize that it is possible that the Cremona Document turns out to be nothing but an elaborate hoax. But it is also possible that this story changes our understanding of American history. If so, we will have Scott and Janet to thank.

PREFACE
By Scott Wolter

Before reading this book, it is important for me to address certain challenges that have arisen since this research journey began back in 2006. First, the vast amount of material that has come forward, especially since May of 2017, has been immensely complicated and difficult to figure out where it all fits into the overall story that has unfolded. Each new set of documents has presented its own unique set of challenges raising questions that have been difficult to answer with some never being resolved to the author's satisfaction. I have questions about certain documents and things that have transpired both in the field and with certain aspects of the written material and artifacts.

I would be remiss if I didn't point out the obvious "yellow flags" that have appeared as myself and others have researched both the Cremona Document material, and the Sinclair/Wemyss journals first brought forward to me in July of 2016. Regarding the Sinclair/Wemyss journals, the first yellow flag is the person who discovered them, Diana Muir. Anyone with on-line investigative skills will find out that Diana has an interesting past, one that includes embellishing her academic resume, and claiming to possess historical documents she didn't have although this happened over forty years ago.

After critiquing her story of how and where she came into possession of the journals, and then traveling myself to that location, things seemed to check out. Shortly after examining and photographing the lambskin map and book number 19 of 20 written by John Weems Jr., I was impressed by what I saw and had no reason to doubt the veracity of the documents at the time. Shortly thereafter, Diana texted low resolution pictures of six pages of the crew lists that looked convincing and still do. I had grand plans to test the age of the map by running a C-14 test and was looking forward to seeing the rest of the journals Diana claimed she still had but it was not to be. For some reason, she became nervous and said she had thrown the journals into a dumpster.

Fortunately, the video and pictures I took at the I met Diana to at the Mormon Temple in Nauvoo, Illinois, and fortunately, the video and pictures I took of the of the map and John Weems Jr's book survive, along with a few other photos of selected pages, as well as three original pages Diana had put away prior to throwing everything else away.

Because of Diana's past and mystifying claim of throwing the potentially history-changing documents away (part of me wants to believe she still has them somewhere), many have questioned the veracity of the journals and understandably so. That said, we have done our best to vet the content and while there still are many questions, it is hard for us to believe that Diana, or anyone else, could have created the vast historical story that spans over 400 years and fifteen generations of the Sinclair and Wemyss Scottish clans.

Similar suspicion has been raised by outside researchers about Don Ruh. Some are suggesting that he created the Cremona Document material. Still others claim Bill Jackson never existed.

Truth be told, Bill Jackson is a shadowy figure whose history is nearly impossible to track down. One reason is Bill's father was arrested in the 1930s for raising money to be sent to the Irish Republican Army while he was living in the United States. He was given the option of going to jail or turning state witness and changing his identity to avoid a prison sentence. Having a wife and young son (Bill) he chose the latter. This is why an internet search me and others did many years ago looking for information about Bill when first vetting Don's story came up empty. That said, I am still convinced Bill Jackson was a real person who did indeed die in 2000 after a lengthy battle with Parkinson's disease and arteriosclerosis. Because of the work Don, Bill, and others did for the company they worked for, they tended to keep a very low profile. I have seen only three pictures Don has identified as Bill Jackson and have no reason to believe they are not him. Don also wrote a lengthy history about his relationship with his best friend in his book, *The Scrolls of Onteora*.[1] Granted, pictures and information about Bill Jackson are sparse, but given his occupation with the company he worked for and his family name being changed as child, it shouldn't come as a big surprise he is somewhat of a mysterious figure.

Of course, any investigator worth a grain of salt will also look very closely at Donald Ruh and as part of my due diligence, I did just that. Similar suspicion

---

1 Ruh, Don, *Scrolls of Onteora*, Pages 23-29.

has been raised by outside researchers about Don Ruh. Some are suggesting that he created the Cremona Document material while others believe that Don and Diana colluded together on Diana's journals which is impossible. I introduced Diana to Don via email in late 2017 who helped him publish his book on-line. Diana didn't know who Don was when she first shared her translations and transcriptions of the journals with me in July of 2016.

I think it's important to share my experience with Don in 2020/2021 during the Covid outbreak: one day, an envelope arrived at our home that was stuffed with roughly one-hundred pages that was sent by Don. After opening the package and pulling out the pages, I noticed the familiar words "Top Secret" at the top of each page. I had seen a few of these reports over the years that Don had shared with me about missions he and his colleagues had performed at the behest of our government. I called Don and asked what was going on. He said, "You read the material, do not make copies, and when you're done, send it back and I'll send you the next batch." This consisted of five batches of over 500 pages of reports which lasted for nearly a year and a half. I share this story to give the reader confidence that I know as well as anyone still living, the nature of the work Don, Bill, and the rest of the company personnel performed as paid contractors who did often dangerous work that helped keep our country safe. Anyone who reads these reports knows all the people who worked for the company were intelligent, crafty, and clever including Bill Jackson and Donald Ruh.

While I consider Don to be a very close friend, I also know he understands the important historical implications of the Cremona Document and the need to carefully vet every aspect of it to ensure the information presented is accurate and true to the very best of our ability. This requires a close, careful, and critical look at everything and everyone involved, including Don Ruh. When we first met and began working on what we then called, "Bill Jackson's material", we assumed the material given to Don by Bill's son, Mark Jackson, and the two floppy disks found hidden behind the picture Bill had given Don, were the extent of what was passed on. It wasn't until April of 2017, when Don received the package from Bill's daughter Melissa with the two maps and page one of *A Year We Remember* written in Theban, that we began to realize Bill had not sold everything he had purchased in 1971. Over the course of the next six years, Don received several packages and puzzle boxes from deceased colleagues who had been given Cremona Document material from Bill with strict instructions that upon their deaths it was to go to Don. These have come not without some "yellow flags" that have appeared along the way.

By themselves, the yellow flags are not overly problematic. Collectively, they do raise eyebrows and questions that outside researchers have already noticed. The following is a short list of items other colleagues and I have noticed:

1. A missing leg on the "m" in letters written by multiple company personnel, including Bill and Don, made by a specific word processor. The issue was explained by a manufacturer's defect with the "m" in the plastic cartridge that was present in the dozen or so word processors that were purchased for company employees.

2. Several letters written by multiple company personnel including Bill and Don, with a missing space within the date that seems to be the trait of a single individual's accidental formatting style.

3. Don being present multiple times when inscribed stones were found in the field that seem to be connected to some aspect of the Cremona Document stories. This includes the "Dove Stone" I found along the Neversink River near Hunter Mountain in 2009, and the "In Camera Stone" Don discovered with David Brody that same year.

4. Our cursory handwriting analysis noted similarities in Don's handwriting with handwritten documents purported to be written by Bill Jackson and others. Many of these documents appear to be copies. This begs the question of where are the documents that were copied if this was the case? Of course, not being an expert in handwriting analysis, we need to accept the possibility we are mistaken.

5. Don's uncanny ability to locate items in the field that others miss.

6. The delivery of documents in cleverly made wooden puzzle boxes that have Don's crafting all over them. If correct, this appears to be an effort to enhance the experience of the delivery of the documents. This of course, has no bearing on the veracity of the information contained in the documents, but could rouse the suspicion of skeptics unnecessarily.

7. Don's uncanny ability to decipher complex encrypted messages. Especially when every message is encrypted differently. However,

it must be acknowledged, he did struggle with the 6609-character-long message from Roberta's Trove, and it took 39 years to figure out the anagram cipher phrase in the Zodiac cryptogram.

8. There is also the strange matter of forgetting about his notebook until 2022. It contained detailed notes and drawings about his experiences with Bill Jackson in Newfoundland in 1971, when they found the Twelfth Century scuttled De Sudeley ship. It could also be that the now 81-year-old Don simply forgot about the notebook. At 65, my own memory isn't what it used to be.

I present this list as a forensic scientist and researcher and in the interest of full disclosure and have listed the items that when looked at critically, do raise questions. I have narrated this commentary to move in front of the potential criticism of my research with Don, by those who have seen similar things and asked questions. As a forensic geologist who has performed thousands of material investigations looking at inorganic materials like concrete and rock, it is easier to document facts, interpret those facts, and eventually draw a conclusion. It is much different and a more difficult task to investigate aspects of human motivation. Don, myself, and others have worked very closely on this research. We have done the best we could possibly do to vet the documents, the artifacts, and the individuals that comprise this immensely complicated and challenging story, but there are still many questions that remain. After 15 years of researching this story, we feel it is time to put everything down on paper and create a historical record, even with some questions remaining and our understanding of the events being less than perfect. What I can say with certainty is that, so far, the internal evidence within the documents, and everything we have been able to investigate in the field thus far, supports the veracity of the historical events presented.

I also want to advise the reader to prepare for several redactions of the new maps, cryptograms, all or parts of decoded messages and commentary we do not want to share with *The Curse of Oak Island* show. Publishing this material has the potential of giving the show free content they can use for additional episodes, enabling them to make potentially millions of dollars in advertising revenue. We have reached out to the show in the hopes of possibly negotiating an agreement that would benefit both parties, but they did not respond. Once the show ends, we will publish a second edition of the book without any of the redactions seen here. We hope the reader understands our position in light of our experiences with the show that have been less than positive.

Scott Wolter
March 2024

INTRODUCTION

The idea for this book came in early March of 2023 after I, Scott, had completed a two-week decipherment of four encrypted messages from the vast trove of material we now call the Cremona Document. The four messages were encrypted differently, the longest of which was nearly 1,900 words. This message required a cipher phrase from an anagram of twenty-four letters. The clue to the phrase was within the other three messages, which we had already decoded, and like many other times when we had figured out the cipher phrase from the anagram, it seemed obvious. "The Power of God is within you" was the perfect cipher phrase and occurred within the lengthy message a total of thirteen times. For those new to the history, symbolism, and esoteric aspects of the Knights Templar, the notion of sacred numbers will be a mystery; for those initiated into these aspects of what is collectively called "Templarism", the number thirteen makes all the sense in the world and, in fact, is to be expected in a legitimate document connected to the Order.

To our surprise, all four encrypted documents in this cache included detailed information about the history of the activities and treasures hidden on Oak Island in Mahone Bay, Nova Scotia. The information included was more detailed than any documents about the island and its secret treasure, and so we knew it had to be legitimate. We also knew Oak Island was only one of many islands and other locations in North America where the Templars hid treasures and artifacts dating back to the late twelfth century. However, along with gold, silver, jewels, and other valuables, there were certain relics brought over from Europe and the Middle East that were coveted above all the rest. Relics like the biological remains of important historical figures and religious artifacts dating back to the time of Christ and beyond. Historians and amateurs alike have for centuries pondered the existence of relics connected to the Arthurian legends and mysteries associated with the Knights Templar and where they might be today. It turns out not only do these important religious relics exist and made their way to North America, but two of the most revered and coveted historical artifacts in history spent time on Oak Island. This was a huge surprise to both of us and prompted the writing of this book, which we felt needed to be a separate work from the manuscript we had already begun, which tells the full story of the Cremona Document and the voluminous material Don received from his deceased colleagues. This story is incredible, and everyone who reads this book also needs to read these books: *The Scrolls of Onteora: The Cremona Document*, and *The Cryptic Code of the Templars in America: Origins of the Hooked X™*, and look for the upcoming book *The Templar Covenant in America: The Truth About the Hooked X™*.

We are sure people are wondering about the origins of the documents in Bill Jackson's collection, documents that now belong to Donald Ruh—Bill's best friend and colleague from their days working together at a private security company:

During an overseas visit, Bill Jackson purchased a document he tracked down in Rome from a member of a prominent Italian family, Gustave Benvenuto. Once the encrypted document was deciphered, it told the tale of the treasures and documents the Templars recovered (not discovered) under the South Wall of the Temple in Jerusalem, circa 1118. The recovered documents led to a late twelfth-century mission by the Templars to North America, in what is now the Catskill Mountains in upstate New York, to recover ancient scrolls hidden at a place called the Temple of the Goddess. This story inspired Bill to invite Don to join him in a search for one of six ships lost on the southern coast of Newfoundland during the expedition to recover the scrolls between 1178-1180. Incredibly, Bill and Don found the remains of the scuttled ship proving to Bill the document he had purchased was legitimate. Six years later, after hiking the Catskills searching for the Temple of the Goddess and the tomb of Altomara, the female navigator of the expedition who was killed during a skirmish with indigenous tribes and buried inside a small cave sealed with a large boulder, they found the cave and Altomara's remains.

After abandoning writing a book about the document and his adventures with Don over his frustration with close-minded academics, Bill decided to write a novel he never finished due to his diagnosis with Parkinson's disease and arterial sclerosis. In 1994, he made the decision to sell the document to an agent of the Roman Catholic Church named Archbishop Paul Marcinkus. Bill passed away in 2000. In 2004, his son Mark signed an agreement turning over all of his father's Cremona Document research and the rights to the stories over to Don.

After our meeting in 2006, Don contacted me to help hike up Hunter Mountain to the Temple of the Goddess where, using one of the Cremona Document maps, they found a shallowly buried, inscribed stone. In 2017, Don received the first of several packages and wooden puzzle boxes from his deceased colleagues. This led to the realization that Bill had pulled the most important parts of the Cremona Document—including several maps, letters, and reports—and disseminated them to his trusted colleagues at the private security company that all had worked for with strict instructions these items should go to Don upon their deaths.

From 2017 to 2023, four of Bill and Don's colleagues—John Drake, John Lennon, Dan Spartan, and David Rian—passed away leaving a total of six packages or puzzle boxes of material for Don that originally came from Bill Jackson. The details about the delivery and contents of these packages are discussed in *The Templar Covenant in America: The Truth About the Hooked X™*, but the only thing in the vast trove of documents that Don received from his deceased friends that had anything to do with Oak Island was the Neck Map found in the Spartan Box discussed in Chapter 5.

It has been an incredibly wild and exhilarating ride for both of us and we are excited to share the stories in the encrypted messages that directly relate to the 228-year-old legend of buried treasure on Oak Island that came to us in the first two months of 2023.

We feel it is noteworthy that as this book is published the immensely popular cable television show on History, *The Curse of Oak Island*, will have aired for an amazing eleven seasons. Rick and Marty Lagina are the two brothers whose quest has been to find the legendary treasure that has had other treasure hunters searching the island, and various archives, for well over two centuries. Both of us have had personal experiences with the show, that in their own weird way have led each of us to this point. What we both know is one of the world's most fascinating and captivating mysteries has finally been solved once and for all. What we also know is the truth behind the enduring mystery is even better than anyone could have possibly imagined. We hope you enjoy this story as much as we have enjoyed living it.

CHAPTER 1:

THE HISTORY OF
THE OAK ISLAND MYSTERY

Before sharing our experiences, it is important to share the history of the Oak Island mystery to give proper context for what is to follow. Geologically, the "island" was actually two islands after the Laurentide Ice Sheet melted away in the northern hemisphere approximately 10,000 years ago. The roughly one-mile-long by a little less than one-half-mile wide parcels of land totaling 140 acres, were divided by a shallow swampy area that was partially filled in by erosion and people when in 1965 a road was constructed from the mainland and along the southern side connecting the two land formations. As you will see on one of our recently acquired maps, the island was drawn as two islands, clearly predating construction of the road. Legend has it, in the summer of 1795, a teenaged boy named Daniel McGinnis was exploring the island during a fishing trip, when he noticed a depression in the ground and a block and tackle in a tree. The next day he returned with friends and shovels and pickaxes, and started digging. Shortly thereafter they discovered the wooden remains of a man-made shaft, and the legend was born.

With Oak Island's reputation for being a haven to pirates, stories grew out of the remains of what were thought to be ancient workings where a fabulous treasure was hidden and might still remain somewhere underground. McGinnis and his friends dug down to the water table and stopped when water flooded their hole, but that was only the beginning of the digging that followed over the next two-plus centuries, into the hole that became known as the "Money Pit".

PIRATE AGE

One of the most popular and plausible theories about who could have hidden treasure at Oak Island is pirates. The Pirate Age was in full swing on the high seas primarily in the Atlantic and Indian Oceans for roughly seventy-five years between 1660 and 1735, and some speculate many pirates had ties to the descendants of the fugitive Knights Templar. Pirates like Henry Morgan (1635-1688), William Kidd (Circa 1700), Calico Jack (1682-1720), Blackbeard (Circa 1718), and Samuel Bellamy (1689-1717) were famous for pillaging vulnerable ships primarily from Europe. The most famous pirate name associated with the Oak Island treasure is Captain William Kidd (1645 – 1701) who famously pillaged the Atlantic and Indian oceans in the 1690s. Kidd was eventually captured and hanged in 1701. His body was then hung in a gibbet at the mouth of the Thames River in England as a reminder to would-be pirates of what happens to those who defy the law.

MARIE ANTOINETTE JEWELS

Another popular theory is about when Marie Antoinette and King Louis XVI escaped from Paris, France, and disappeared with the crown jewels in 1791. She and the king were captured later that year, and she was beheaded for treason in 1793. Her story is a tragic tale and one that is filled with deceit and betrayal. The Oak Island connection grew out of speculation that she and her husband Louie had fled to North America and hidden the jewels on Oak Island before their capture. The "Crown Jewels" story that became legend is highly unlikely due the timing of their escape in 1791 and the beginning of the Oak Island mystery in 1795—incidentally an era of heavy ship traffic in Mahone Bay and Halifax harbor, making this theory a long shot at best.

KNIGHTS TEMPLAR AND THE HOLY GRAIL

Another immensely popular suspect to have been involved in burying treasure on Oak Island is the medieval order of monks who were disbanded by the Roman Catholic Church and the King of France, also known as Philip the Fair, on October 13, 1307. The Knights Templar were known to have immense wealth, religious artifacts, and the finest sailing fleet in the world at that time. It is also known that a fleet of Templar ships loaded with treasure at the western port of LaRochelle in France, disappeared into history the night before the King of France and the Church arrested, tortured, and eventually burned the Templars on October 13, 1307, a date that became known for bad luck on "Friday the 13th". This legend has persisted for over 700 years, and we now know the story to be true. We also know where the Templars hid their treasures for decades in Scotland before bringing a large cache to Nova Scotia and burying them at multiple locations, including Oak Island.

SAMUEL BALL

Samuel Ball was born into slavery in 1765 on a plantation in South Carolina. Toward the end of the Revolutionary War, the British became desperate for bodies and offered young black men freedom and the promise of land after the war to fight for the crown. Despite losing to the colonists, Ball survived the war and was granted land for cabbage farming in Sherburne and Chester, Nova Scotia in 1784. He was a very successful businessman and purchased more land, eventually acquiring parcels in Mahone Bay, including a small plot on Oak Island in 1787 that slowly grew to thirty-six acres.[1]

Legend has it, Ball was adamant about buying lot twenty-four on the island, paying much more than the going rate for land elsewhere in the area. Did he know something about the island's history others did not? He was certainly aware of the legend of hidden treasure and may have been the first to secretly dig for it. One possibility of where he may have learned about the treasure hidden by the ideological descendants of the Templars is through another man named Samuel Ball whose name appears in the Sinclair/ Wemyss journals in 1770. John Weems Jr. kept detailed journals about his involvement in the "Covenant"—the four-centuries-long, father-to-son tradition of checking on the sites where Templar treasure was hidden by Earl Henry Sinclair and his men in 1395 and 1398. Fifteen generations were part of the Covenant to establish what they called "A Free Templar State" in North America—five of the Sinclair Clan and ten of the Wemyss-Weems Clan—which eventually become the United States of America.

---

1 https://www.blaze.tv/series/curse-oak-island/mystery-samuel-ball

On May 14, 1769, John received a message from his father asking him to come see him as soon as possible:

> *A courier arrived today from Philadelphia and my father has requested that I return home to deal with an important family matter. My father has never asked anything of me before, so I feel obligated to attend. He has insisted that I stop in Staunton and solicit Brother John Scott to accompany me as Mother has been ill and she wishes to see him. My brother-in-law Richard Gott and sister Margaret have agreed to look after Kitty and my small family in my absence. I hope to be gone only a few weeks and will leave in the morrow to do his bidding.*

Then 28-year-old John Weems Jr. left his farm in Hillsboro, North Carolina, and after a week of travel arrived in Abington, Pennsylvania to meet with his father. Once there, he was told about the Covenant and that it was his turn to travel with two elder Freemasons to check on the treasure sites to ensure their safety. On May 24, 1769, he recorded his thoughts:

> *It has taken hours to put my hand to pen and write my thoughts. I now understand why Father has taught us to write our thoughts each evening. Not only do we chronicle the events in our lives, but he has been preparing us for the adventure ahead. When I asked why he did not invite my brother Thomas he replied that although he loved his sons equally Thomas is a slave owner and might be swayed by the prospects of riches. Whereas I, am satisfied with my life and do not seek to put myself above other men. I am not certain that I agree with his assessment but will try to do my best to fulfill his wishes.*
>
> *Father has always taught us that we are the descendants of great kings and queens in Scotland. Father is the grandson of the Earl of Wemyss, the Grandmaster of the Freemasons in Edinburgh. As such he bears the responsibility of a great family. When Thomas and I were of age we were initiated into the Freemasons in Philadelphia and so began our training in trades that would benefit both our country and our lives. I have been trained as a surveyor and engineer while Thomas claims his occupation as a blacksmith and metal worker. We are both educated men although our interests differ.*

Father's story of our families' involvement in Freemason activities is confusing and lengthy. He has promised that as I read the journals of my ancestors who have gone before me that I will begin to understand the enormity of my journey. He has put into my safekeeping a small chest of journals that reach back hundreds of years requesting that I begin with the oldest. It is only then that I will understand what the Freemasons and the Templars before them have kept hidden and the efforts taken to preserve it. The Brethren have always kept such secrets and I have heard rumors for years but have given them no heed until now.

Father is concerned with the current political happenings and has received word that settlers have begun to settle the area of Nova Scotia where we must travel. He has arranged for us to leave on board ship in the morrow for Cape Breton where we are to seek out an alliance with others who would support our cause. My Uncle John Scott will accompany me as he did my father many years ago and acquaint me with the hiding place of what Father refers to only as the Covenant. He has also demanded that I record my journey so that someday I may pass the responsibility along to my own son.

The journey begins.

Upon completing the task and returning to Abington, John Weems Sr. said his son needed to assemble a group of men, all Freemasons[2], to go again the following spring to recover those treasures. On June 29, 1769, John Jr. once again put his thoughts to paper in an historic journal entry that will likely become famous:

Father has arrived home and is pleased to see us. He asked for a report of our findings and Brother John reported that all sites were undisturbed and protected. He told Father of the men we had met with and the places we had visited. Father also asked for a report of political affairs in Boston and in Nova Scotia. Brother John stated that events were unpredictable, and it seems as if both countries are on the verge of war. Father agrees and stated that he had been meeting with the Brethren in Philadelphia about the unrest concerning England

---

2 https://www.freemason.com/what-is-freemasonry/

and France. He now has more to ask of me, being pleased that I gladly accepted instruction from Brother Scott on our trip to Cape Breton and Nova Scotia with few complaints.

I repeated my doubts about the journals to my father and he responded; "My grandfather's grandfather and his grandfather before him saw the treasure with his own eyes and helped to move it to the colonies. They wanted to ensure that it was safe and protected until a free nation could be built where God's children could flourish in the bosom of Abraham." He instructed me to be faithful and obey the admonishments of he and the Brethren. He promised that God would direct me in my actions if only I have faith.

Father has told me of his meeting with the Brethren; John Hanson of Maryland, George Mason of Mason's Island, Arthur Sinclair, Ebenezer Morton, William Irvine, Nathaniel Gorham of Massachusetts, and Joseph Dickinson this past year. They plan to move the treasure and artifacts to Mason's Island where they are preparing a vault to hold them. It will my job to organize a caravan of 6 wagons and suitable Brethren to assist in moving the treasure to Mason's Island where the Brethren will be able to defend it. They are afraid they will lose access to the sites where it is hidden if the British should win the ensuing war. He stated that all of these men and their families were part of the Covenant and would do their best to aid me in my task.

I am distressed that I will be unable to accomplish this, but Father says I am well prepared and should enlist my brother Thomas for suitable wagons and labor. He gives me 7 maps that he has copied onto unused paper and tells me that each group of 4 or 5 men should reclaim the treasure at each location. Each map is marked with the latitude and marked as to where the treasure resides. I have already visited the islands and will (be) able to direct them on whom to speak with and where to begin. We are to load the wagons with trade goods for the natives and people of Halifax to justify our journey. He has also included instructions on how find the last island in western New York, having enlisted the help of Ebenezer Morton. He has asked that I make this journey myself as I must travel through the land of the Onondowaga.

To complete this task, I must take into my confidence those brethren that I trust the most. Father says he trusts my judgment that I will be able to recruit these men in a timely fashion. He has directed me to the Grand Master of the North Carolina Lodge. He suggests that we leave in the spring to recover the treasure and bring it by wagon caravan to Maryland. Brother Hanson and Brother Irvine will assist in ferrying it to Mason's Island in the nearby river.

The candle is dimming and about to go out. I must retire although I know I cannot sleep. Tomorrow I will begin my journey home with Brother Scott. I pray that the Holy Father and Holy Mother protect and direct me in this task. I also pray that my wife Kitty will understand another absence.

After a long winter of recruitment and planning, John Jr. and his other brother, Bartholomew, traveled again to Abington to meet with his father. In addition to a total forty-six brethren, they also brought along six slaves who were to be given their "manumission", or freedom. upon completion of the mission.[3] On April 6, 1770, John Jr. explains how in addition to bringing twenty men, his brother also brought six slaves, one of them was named Samuel Ball:

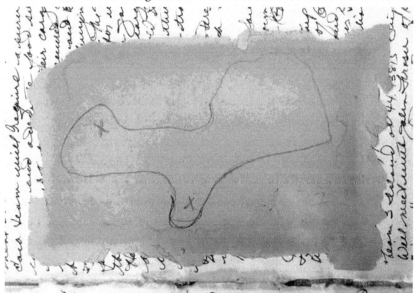

Between the pages of book #2 of John Weems Jr's journals was an old paper map of McNabb Island with two "X's" marking the locations of treasure hidden in 1398 that have since been recovered. (Wolter, 2016)

3 https://www.merriam-webster.com/dictionary/manumission

My blood brother Bartholomew has arrived with a retinue of 20 men and 4 wagons of tobacco for trade with the natives in Nova Scotia. He brings with him 6 slaves for whom he has papers of manumission so that they may be released to freedom after we have completed our journey.

John Jr. specifically mentions Samuel Ball in an entry on May 5, 1770. Ball tells John Jr. his brother has treated him well and will miss him as a free man.

"We have arrived at the manor and Father and Mother are excited to see us, especially Bartholomew who has been absent for 6 years. We camp outside by the barns and the men are excited for a day or two of rest. The horses have been released into the fields after a visit to the farrier and the wagons are sheltered in the barns against any rain or bad weather. Samuel Ball one of Thomas's freed slaves whom he has trained as a blacksmith has taken over Father's forge and with the help of the other men is strengthening the wagon wheels and wagon tongues against the rough roads ahead. Thomas has treated his slaves well and I find them well trained and able to read and write. Samuel tells me that Master Thomas and his mistress Elizabeth has provided a school and church for them and that he will miss them both."

This fascinating entry reveals important clues that shed light on the burning question of whether this recently freed slave who helped recover Templar treasure in Nova Scotia, is the same Samuel Ball who purchased lots on Oak Island. The short answer is no, but there still could be a connection between the two men and the treasures both knew were there. Samuel Ball who purchased several lots on Oak Island lived from 1765 to 1846. We also know he first arrived in Nova Scotia in 1784 at the age of 19, and first purchased lots on Oak Island in 1787 when he was 22. The other freed slave named Samuel Ball who helped recover treasures in Nova Scotia was obviously an adult to have been trained as a blacksmith. At the youngest, he was possibly 16 years of age which is still 12 years older than the other Samuel Ball who was only 4 years-old in 1769.

This incredible coincidence of having two slaves named Samuel Ball living at the same time and involved in recovering treasure in Nova Scotia is astonishing. Even though they were not the same person, it begs curiosity to wonder if there were any other connections. During this tragic time of slave ownership in American History, slaves routinely took the family name of their owners. This is known to be true of the Samuel Ball of Oak Island who was born and raised on a plantation in South Carolina. The other Samuel Ball—who lived in North Carolina and was owned by Thomas Weems who inherited him from the Redfern plantation—was likely owned by a man named Ball before Thomas. While it is certainly possible the two had different

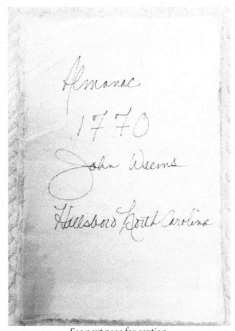

See next page for caption.

owners with the same last name, it is also possible they were both born on a plantation owned by the same man, who owned property in both states.

It is amazing to have two African American slaves with the same name, living most of their lives during the same time, and to also be involved in recovering Templar treasures in Nova Scotia. In fact, Oak Island resident and farmer, Samuel Ball, is listed as a co-discoverer of treasure in the "Money Pit" in a book written by Mather Byles Desbrisay, titled, *The History of Lunenburg County, Nova Scotia*, published in 1870.[4] Whether this claim is true will be addressed in the coming pages.

FRANKLIN DELANO ROOSEVELT

The thirty-second President of the United States, and a Freemason, was another well-known person who was captivated with the Oak Island buried treasure story.[5] He was an investor in a company committed to finding the treasure that was formed in April of 1909 called, The Old Gold Salvage & Wrecking Compa-

---

4   https://books.google.com/books?id=_qgOAAAAYAAJ&printsec=frontcover&source=gbs_ge_summary_r&cad=0#v=onepage&q&f=false
5   https://www.freemason.com/franklin-d-roosevelt-freemason/

This page and previous. The cover of book #3 of John Weems Jr's journals is made of linen paper and contains a page with information about one of John's brothers, Thomas', freed slaves named Samuel Ball. He was trained as a blacksmith and while he lived during the same time period as Samuel Ball who owned property on Oak Island, they are not the same person. (Wolter, 2016) ny.[6] Then twenty-seven-year-old Roosevelt (1882-1945) and a group of treasure hunters traveled to Oak Island in 1909 and spent the months from August until November digging to no avail. The company lasted until 1912 and was dissolved. Roosevelt maintained a life-long interest in the Oak Island mystery until his death 1945. Other famous people who have invested money in the hope of finding treasure on the island include Errol Flynn and John Wayne. Wayne was a well-known Freemason and may have heard rumors floating within Masonic circles that piqued his interest.[7] In light of what we now know about the connections of the Founding Fathers' involvement in the recovery of the Earl Henry Sinclair treasures, and other treasures hidden in the late fourteenth century, it is plausible he received information that was beyond just rumor.

This picture of members of The Old Gold Salvage & Wrecking Company was taken on Oak Island in the summer of 1909. A then twenty-seven-year-old Theodore Delano Roosevelt (smoking a pipe) was part of the group that spent several months looking for treasure they never found. (Internet)

Dan Blankenship

Shortly after reading a 1965 Reader's Digest article about the legend and the four men who died searching for treasure that same year, Blankenship and his wife moved from Florida to Nova Scotia. He then spent the next fifty years searching for the treasure on the island and became the affable patriarch of the mystery till his death in 2019.

6 https://www.oakislandtours.ca/the-old-gold-salvage-and-wrecking-company.html
7 https://scottishritenmj.org/blog/freemason-john-wayne

LAGINA BROTHERS

Most people who know anything about the Oak Island mystery are aware of the hit History Channel show *The Curse of Oak Island*. Like Dan Blankenship, Marty and Rick Lagina became fascinated with the Oak Island story after reading the same Reader's Digest article from 1965. They began their quest for treasure in 2006 when they purchased a controlling interest in Oak Island Tours who owned the majority of the island. Since that time, they have spent vast amounts of money searching for the treasure and then hit pay dirt, literally, when the cable television show premiered in January of 2014. After airing for eleven seasons and ripping the island apart with excavations and endless drilling, the brothers have become famous and very wealthy due to fantastic ratings for the well-produced show that still has viewers captivated even though it is now abundantly clear there is nothing left to find. The longevity of this show speaks volumes as to the lure and fascination of the possibility of finding treasure, regardless of how unlikely the circumstances may be.

THE "CURSE" OF OAK ISLAND

Perhaps the most famous legend associated with the Oak Island mystery is the curse that a seventh person must die before the treasure can be found. Most people today believe the "Curse" story was invented by the *Curse of Oak Island* show, but that is not true. While the show has certainly capitalized on the legend by constantly reminding viewers during each episode, the origin of the curse dates to the tragic loss of four lives on the island in 1965. This was the year Robert Restall Sr. entered the Money Pit shaft not realizing natural poisonous gas, likely methane, had filled shaft causing Restall to pass out. Realizing his father was in trouble, his son went into the shaft to rescue his father but also fell unconscious. Compounding the tragedy, their colleagues Cyril Hitz, Carl Graeser, and another worker named Andy DeMont all went into the shaft to try and rescue the Restalls but only DeMont got out alive.

Two lives had previously been lost searching for treasure, Maynard Kaiser was killed after falling into an excavation pit, and another person died around 1860. It was the loss of these six souls that serve as the basis of the legend of a curse that likely began shortly after the 1965 tragedy.

A granite memorial was erected to the six men who died searching for treasure on Oak Island. The six deaths serve as the basis for the legend of a curse made famous by the "Curse of Oak Island." The made-up legend says the seventh person associated with the search "must die" before the treasure will be found. The death of Dan Blankenship in 2019 could be argued is that seventh person, yet discovery of the treasure remains elusive. (Wolter, 2008)

"Seven Must Die"

For those reading this that are diehards for the *Curse of Oak Island* show we would be remiss if we didn't address the tagline, "Seven Must Die", used to deepen the mystery of the show, that in reality was a complete fabrication. The basis for the so-called curse is listed previously. However, the production company, Prometheus Entertainment, dreamed up the idea of an ongoing curse that fueled macabre interest by claiming the treasure would only be found after a seventh person involved in searching for treasure died, thus ending the "curse". This made-for-TV idea was a central part of the buildup for each episode of the show for at least seven of the show's ten seasons. However, the curse mantra has quietly disappeared from the show since Dan Blankenship passed away in 2019. His death, and others that have transpired since the fabricated curse came into use are described below.

Dan Blankenship (1923-2019)

If anyone would qualify for the seventh person to die for the treasure to be found it would be Dan. And no, he did not die under mysterious circumstances or while engaged in the search for the treasure, but his name has become synonymous with the Oak Island mystery. Despite his passing and the four years of searching, the Lagina brothers and their supporters are no closer to finding treasure—other than the millions of dollars they make annually on the show—than when they began their search. The reason for this is obvious and will become self-evident as you continue reading. It's interesting the show stopped using the "Seven Must Die" in their marketing after Blankenship died. Perhaps out of respect for Dan and how silly a premise it was in the first place. It falls under the category of something that seemed like a good idea at the time and while it surely generated interest early on, as more people involved with the show passed away and the seasons piled up, it lost its appeal.

Matt Chisholm (1983-2014)

Shortly after *The Curse of Oak Island* show premiered in 2014, a producer named Matt Chisholm died under mysterious circumstances. He was reportedly found dead in his room only a few hours after reportedly receiving a tip about a map of Oak Island allegedly connected to Freemasonry. Curiously, the show never publicly acknowledged the death of Chisholm which seems odd since the death of a vital member of a film crew would have been devastating. Because I have worked closely with a film crew for several years shooting a television show, I understand how close knit a group becomes working on the road for many months at a time. Losing a member of your crew is like losing a family member and acknowledging the tragedy is the least that should happen and honoring such a loss should be assumed.

Why didn't the show at least acknowledge the death of one of their own? Was it to preserve the "Seven Must Die" curse story used to entice viewers to tune in? It would seem so since the thirty-one-year-old Chisholm was definitely part of the Oak Island search team as a producer, but apparently his mysterious death was too early in the show's run, and the network and the production company likely feared it would bring scrutiny to the marketing idea of a curse they were committed to. After almost ten years, the treasure still hasn't been found and appears to call into question the veracity of the so-called curse.

Fred Nolan (1927-2016)

Anyone with a strong interest in the Oak Island mystery will know the name Fred Nolan.[8] Fred was a land surveyor who lived on the island and was interested in the legend for over fifty years of his life until he died in 2016 at the age of eighty-eight. He did extensive research and is credited with discovering a large cross made of glacial boulders on his property that many people believed was related to the treasure hidden on the island. Dubbed "Nolan's Cross" the show spent two episodes in season four hoping it pointed to where the lost treasure was located. Predictably, no treasure was ever found using the cross which one could also argue was a series of natural boulders in the shape of a cross that was made by melting glaciers at the end of the last ice age, and not by the hands of people.

While his death was not related to an accident during his search for treasure on the island, a case could be made that because of his half-century involvement he was the seventh person to die. However, it is alleged a tragedy must happen during *digging* operations for the curse to end and the treasure to finally be revealed. By the time readers reach the end of this book the whole Oak Island story will be revealed, and no one has to die to get there.

---

8 https://en.wikipedia.org/wiki/Frederick_G._Nolan#Oak_Island

Don Ruh holds the brass device he discovered inside a decorative ornament that was blown off Bannerman Island. He found this in the summer of 1968 near the very spot where he is standing. (Wolter, 2022)

CHAPTER 2

THE BACKGROUND OF
THE CREMONA DOCUMENT
& SINCLAIR/WEMYSS JOURNALS

Before jumping into the Oak Island aspects of the overall story, we need to look at the most relevant background information, so the new material specific to what happened on the island makes sense. It all began in 1968 when Don Ruh and his childhood friend, Bill Jackson, were scuba diving and swimming off the shores of Bannerman Island in the Hudson River.[9] Francis Bannerman IV (1851-1918) was an arms dealer of Scottish descent who died in 1918 leaving his estate—with munitions stored there—to fall into ruins.[10] In 1920, an estimated 200 tons of black powder exploded destroying parts of the castle and sending the munitions into the river. Don, Bill, and other friends were fishing near the island when Don found two decorative ornaments on the shore of the mainland across from the island. Don gave the ornaments to Bill who later discovered two items that had been hidden inside one of them: a clay tube containing two parchments sealed with beeswax, later discovered to contain a highly controversial biblical-era message, and a hockey-puck sized brass device containing four metal inserts.

The brass device had strange symbols etched onto the surface which were later realized to be Theban script, which is known to have been used by

---

9 https://bannermancastle.org/history/
10 https://www.findagrave.com/memorial/8048322/francis-bannerman

the medieval order of the Knights Templar. The turning point was the name "Altomara" etched onto one of the metal inserts that ultimately led Bill Jackson to Rome where he purchased what we now call the Cremona Document, from a prominent Italian family named Benvenuto, in 1971. The document contained maps, letters, and several encrypted messages and reports Bill was able to decipher over the next two years. The largest report was a deposition taken from Sir Ralph De Sudeley, the leader of a Templar mission to North America to recover ancient scrolls hidden at a site called the Temple of the Goddess in the Catskill Mountains. The story of the recovery of the documents was recorded by two Cistercian monks, one for the Order of the Temple (Knights Templar), and one for the Roman Catholic Church, in Seborga, Italy, in 1180 upon De Sudeley's return to Europe.

We wrote our own commentaries about the recovery of treasure and artifacts under the South Wall circa 1118, and the De Sudeley deposition, in our own books and strongly recommend them for those interested in reading more. This book is not intended to be a rehash of our past work. Our

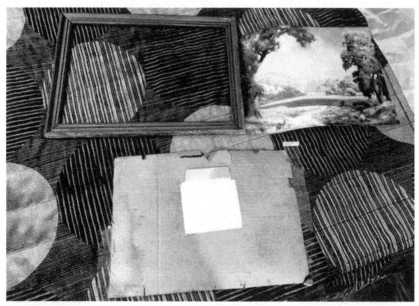

The picture Bill Jackson gave to Don in 1994 had two floppy discs and the "Compass and Square" map. The print was originally painted by American artist Robert Atkinson Fox (1860-1935) in the 1920s and is titled, "Glorious Vista." One of the floppy discs contained a typed version of the deposition given by Sir Ralph De Sudeley after he returned from North America to Seborga, Italy. The story relayed by De Sudeley was encrypted using Theban symbols and a cipher phrase of "Aelis Capitolina." (Wolter, 2021)

intent is to bring our investigation into the Oak Island aspects of the Cremona Document into proper context in relation to the overall story. De Sudeley's narrative about his journey to North America from 1177-1180 is titled, *A Year We Remember*, and is required reading. In 2008 Don discovered two floppy disks behind a framed print that Bill Jackson had given him many years prior. On one of them was an already decoded version of *A Year We Remember*, in English. Bill gave the print to Don without ever telling him what he had done.

A Year We Remember

We have followed the writing found to be in the Theban alphabet translated to Greek and Ivri from Adoniram's scrolls that were found below the stables of Solomon to Palmyra and have the devices with us. The ancient maps show a land of Onteora far to the west, but the route is far from certain. With the round disks we can read some of the ancient scrolls that reveal how the unclean fled to Tigwa and set sail for the Kingdoms of Woton far to the North. To the place in the past where the Goddess commanded the outcasts of Solomon to erect a temple in her honor in the land of Onteora. There they hid the ancient writings, the secrets of the ages, the facts about our [L]ord.

The disk is the key to unlock these. The North Finder and Star Finder will help plot the way laid out in the sailor's loop but to read it we must seek the help of the King of the North.

We sail in the spring from Luongo for Esbjerg. We make landfall at Dunwich Engeolnde to receive funds and the bishop's blessing and stay in the Templar Hostelry near the church of St. Peters, but the Celt and the Spaniard seek rooms in the local tavern because of the nearness of the Blackfriars [Dominican monks]. There is but one horse at the Hostelry and it has a bruised leg, but the Spaniard made poultice of Fenugreek and by the morrow it is well enough for me to ride to my kinfolk. I stop at Shropshire for the hammersmith to make a copy of the discs. It is crude work but will be good for use. We will stay a fortnight [14 days] awaiting the storms to abate. The Celt has found an Anam Cara whom he shares with the Spaniard and are quite content. So much for the vow of celibacy.

...at the Court of the King of the North and are well received. We are here introduced to a priestess of the Goddess named Altomara and the Spaniard is besotted with her much to our shame, but the King is not offended. She leads us to the quay and states, "Fater Kat Bot" Lion(e)l translates as he is a cousin of the queen and speaks some of their talk, "Father gives a boat." It is a long craft of the North with two decks one below the other, a high prow adorned with a symbol of the Goddess and one strong mast. Altomara states she has been to the Temple before and will guide us, but she says we must leave soon as the North waters will ice up.

We must also ask permission of the local people [Native Americans] to pass through their land and we stock up with some odd items for them. There is beads of colors, axes, kettles, and wool blankets. There is an ongoing mistrust with some of the local people as the Temple is within a place sacred to them but so far, no open hostility. The wind will take us most of the way and we will make landfall once at a place they have a settlement to take on fresh water and food. So, our year begins with Beltane. To follow the loops exactly requires that we start at a place unknown to us so we will make for Gwynedd [Wales] and await favorable winds and then head west by Altomara's course. To appease the priest, the Spaniard takes the priestess to wife. We are all in her hands and she revels in this, but the Spaniard puts her in place. We have provisioned now with six ships and one hundred forty men and women. The women fight with the men and are held equal by them. A strange practice to us.

Aequinoctuim [Latin for Equinox] has passed long since. The Spaniard suffers greatly from the cold, but she keeps him warm as we await one moon past Midsummers Eve. We set sail north by northwest till below the North Star then west as the wind takes us, we make landfall in a fortnight. There are a dozen mud huts here, but the hospitality is warm, and we are well cared for. Here we take on a man called Clyphus who is said to have knowledge of the waters ahead. Two ships remain here. Four now set sail again and we make landfall on an island of oak trees where one ship is to be laden with wood and will return. We have seen no natives of this place. Hubert will return with the copy of the discs and maps of the way thus far. It is insurance.

Again, we set sail but now three days out the wind fails us, and no prayers can set it to blow again. We must take to the oars and pulling the drogue [Funnel shaped device towed behind to slow a ship or pulled to move forward]. *This is a slow and tedious process, but we move after several hours with a northerly current. Fog very heavy settles around us and the Celt and Beaumont set to sending fire arrows aloft as the top of the mast one man sits to see by, but it is in vain as strike solid on rock or ice and have torn a hole in the bottom and are sinking. Both Eldric and I see land and sing out. The other ship takes us in tow and then comes about and pushes us so that we land on a rocky hillside. We take off enough provisions to sustain us and part of the decking from which we will make smaller craft to row to the mainland.*

Night is coming and the other ships fearing a similar fate head out to sea and south. One makes landfall south and west and sets about a fire so that we may take heart from its sight. Altomara takes sky bearings and in the morning, we begin to build rafts. Wood is scarce here. Four days have passed, and three rafts have gone to the other place, but one has not made it, and all were lost Beaumont among them. Eldric the Celt, The Spaniard, Altomara and the one called Clyphus who so far has been of no-good help to us and I set sail in a larger made boat with part of our masts top cut for a mast and sail and reach the other place where we set up to an anchor ashore. Rocks have been laid into the water without fear of her running to ground held fast to the shore by the great round anchor there.

We decide to proceed with the one ship as of the other we have seen nothing since we parted at the sinking of our vessel as it towed it out to deeper water. No sign of our passage must remain. These are not friendly waters. Many fish here and they do not respect strangers to their fishing grounds. We will take the smaller ship we have constructed with its sail and flat bottom behind the other and will reach the mainland in two days' sail with the new wind. First, we round the point and again set ashore on another isle so that Altomara can take sky bearings. There rests an anchor rock here not of our making and we leave below it a record of our passing. The tides are monster.

...ch and are greeted well by the strange inhabitants of the main island. They are of a bronze color tinged reddish are dressed in furs and have various feathers of birds upon their heads. Those with many feathers have higher rank among their peoples. They refer to themselves as "The People" in a language unknown to us. It sounds as Pasa mac quaid ee. They live in houses some thirty feet long of sticks, bark, and mud. There are no windows and a fire in the center makes it very smoke laden. The land is heavily wooded and is teeming with game and birds of many kinds' unknown to us. The deer are much larger than at home and Eldric brings one down with his long bow. The head of these people is much impressed with Eldric's skill with his bow as theirs is shorter, but they are excellent with them and with a weapon of three stones at the ends of three ropes hurled about their heads and thrown. With these they bring down birds of large size.

They are much afraid when we bring off the horses from the ship, but it turns to amazement as no such animal resides here. They will provide us with one hundred dogs to pull our gear, but the wheel is not known to them either and a drag of poles is all that the dogs will pull. We will spend a time with them and when Midsummers Eve has come again Altomara will make her sky measurements for the location of the Temple of Goddess and it is decided that Hubert will return with the ship and twenty and six of us with Eldric, Ishma'il, Lionel, The Spaniard, Clyphus, and Altomara and I will travel first by water then by land over the mountains, beyond the mountains, over the mountains to other mountains, south by west three points less than half the lesser. This is a year we may surely not forget should by the Grace of God and the blessings of the Goddess we survive.

Hubert has taken the ship into a large river and set ashore upon an isle to the left. Upon the right bank, we encounter several hundred of the inhabitants dressed colorfully with bodies painted red and white and black. Altomara states that they are ready for war but when they see me in full armor sword unsheathed facing the rising sun so that it reflects from me, they run away in fear. We cross over in the smaller boat and sound for depth to bring the ship to bear. Then we unload the dogs and the twelve horses, our supplies and we say God speed to our brethren. Hubert set off straight away with the tide and we are alone. Altomara has spoken with the head man of these peoples, and they have word of us. It comes to pass that word travels fast among the different groups here. We are made welcome and learn that it is not us they were expecting to make war on but an enemy to the south. They call themselves the Mikee-Macks [Mi'kmaq] and the daughter of the head man finds Lionel most pleasing. Altomara has spoken to by her mother and some arrangement is come to that she spends time with him but not alone. He is able to provide some communication with her as some of the words of Gwynedd are most similar. I find this most amazing. Her name is Woe-a-tweez- Mita-mu we call her Wasabee.

We agree to aide these peoples in their fight against the enemy. Lionel and Eldric take charge of the battle plans. Eldric charges Wasabee's people to build a wall in a big circle nine chains round with an opening to the east. The wall is of stone three hands thick but at the east only one course on the ground some one hand high. A rod [rod = 16.5 feet] inside the circle he instructs them to dig three trenches a rod or two deep and one wide the length of the opening and several men's feet apart. The women weave from a water plant with wide flat leaves and long slender stalks with a brown seed atop which is good tinder long mats that will cover the trenches on sticks below and with dirt and leaves over them. Behind the west wall on the outside several less deep trenches are constructed but these are not covered with mats only branches and some hides and leaves. In the wood to the north Gertrude the spear maiden sets about some twenty men with spears. Eldric has some two dozen [spear] points he sets upon the poles. These are to lay upon the ground with the men. Clyphus, Adric Galen and I will take some twenty of Wasabee's people and form a phalanx inside the wall behind the trenches. The rest of them are to the south in the wood. The head man sends some of his best to wait in the water and to scout ahead to the south over the river to spy on the advancing army.

Some four hundred of them come over in boats made of bark and wood with a short oar having a thin flat blade on them some thirty men to a boat all painted up and screaming they charge us though the opening lightly jumping over the low rocks and thus pay no heed till they fall into the trenches the next wave jumps this to find themselves into another and so on. Altomara blows a horn of a goat. It makes a long low deep sound and at this Eldric's archers raise up from the outer covered trench to the west and fire volleys into the enemy within. They quickly see that it is a trap and attempt to come around to the west behind Eldric. Then does Gertrude send the spear men at them and our people mounted as cavalry charge them also. At the same time the head man's people set about the guards on the boats and burn them. Then the rest of the people charge as I command our group to move forward. The enemy takes to the water some swimming others in partly burnt boats or those they have put a right. Now a surprise. Eldric blows a horn and from the island comes twenty bark craft pushing a raft ablaze into the retreating boats. Those swimming are clubbed in the water. These people show no quarter. We are victorious.

Alantha Rolf's woman, Galan and Cedric of Londonary have been lost and some dozen of Wasabee's people. More than one hundred of the enemy are dead and many more wounded. They are dispatched but the women are taken as a prize. The circle of stones that was the battle ground rests upon a hill and the village behind it still higher up both overlook a fertile plain. This would be a good place to reside. I have mentioned this in my letters to the Temple and hope that Hubert will not mention it to the Holy Father.

Rolf, Adirc and Sven decide to remain with these people and are accepted into the group. Lionel has eaten the twelve cakes and thus Wasabee travels wither he goes. For his plans and valor in battle there in nothing else I can give him, so I have him kneel and with my sword unsheathed he rises Sir Eldric. The King may not approve but he is far away, and we all recognize him as such. It is the right thing to do."

In a moon [Month or 28 days] we take our leave and with the boat head down the coast stopping each night so that the party ashore with the dogs and horses can regroup. The Al-no-bok's enemies of The People try to steal our horses but we strike a deal with their head man and Lionel leaves his Breast Plate, Shin Guards and Gauntlets with him. They also provide a man called Tamo who will guide us through the many passes as the forest is thick with growth. The wood are so close together in some places a man cannot pass between. Tamo takes us *over a mountainous route, but we see few other of the inhabitants of this land. We come to another large river with a swamp at its mouth and pushing through this bring the horses and dogs over the south side. Here we will abandon the boat taking the sails and some tools with us.*

Then we arrive on the bank of a river with a tall mountain on our right. Altomara states we have come too far. We must go back ten leagues [League ranges in distance between 2.4 to 4.6 statute miles] *north by nine east, but Tamo will go no farther with us. We give him the beast, but it is the only one that remains. We have eaten the rest. The next day we realize that Malcom's cross bow and a quiver of twenty arrows with steel points is missing. We search for them, but they cannot be found. We believe Tamo may have taken them. At the top of this tall mountain is water. This is unusual and Altomara states it is the mountain of a great God of the inhabitants of this land and is sacred to them. There is a large pile of stone here with a clear crystal one at the top with a point worked in its top. South from here we see a rock with a design of the Goddess on it and the name of the people that live here. The three spirals mark a passage of time Eostre. I marveled that they have writing. It is the first I have seen but Altomara and Wasabee tell us these people are not native to the land but live here as guardians of the mountain. We see none of them but feel we are being watched. They are called the Cone* [Cohan?] *or the Elohim.*

When we have gone north and east, we begin to see large stone piles about a rod or two high and all topped with the clear or white shining stone. We follow these as they border a wide road free of brush and trees. We approach a wide river and Lionel goes to cut trees to bridge it, but I cry "Nay" for upon the far bank stands some several hundred of the reddish people and they have many bows, and they suddenly raise a cry of war. I stand forth in armor, but several arrows hit me before they all become silent. Then as one they turn and face an opposing force of tall men in leather vests with a copper-colored plates front and back with many spears with green tips of metal and they all stamp their feet and beat upon drums and cry out. Then a horn as Altomara has is sounded and the spears are lowered to breast height, and they advance to the beat of a drum. These people are fair to look upon with many having blonde hair and blue eyes. The native group break and flee as the phalanx reaches the bank opposite us and one hails Altomara. We are taken aback the language is of that of Gwynedd [Welsh]. We are welcome. These are the people of the Temple of the Goddess. They are stately and tall. The shortest is two heads over me. They are fair of skin with large heads and dress much as we do but have a cloth type robe about their girth that extends over the shoulder.

In the confrontation with the natives one was struck in the chest with an arrow, but the metal plat(e)s caused it to not adhere as did they with my armor. He then used a short spear thrown from a straight stick with a hook at the back and flung much as a catapult. It pierced the throat of the warrior, and he went down. We were taken to the mountain top and shown a structure with a sharp pointed roof made of stone and banked with mud. A wattle wall surrounded it..."

...leaves are turned so we change course and at the sign of the bear we head east. We now enter the land of the Pan Cookie people [Penacook Tribe]. Altomara, Tamo and Wasabee with the Spaniard who is learning their talk go to see their head man. These people are very hungry. The game has fled as there has been no rain for a while, two moons. Our provisions are no less thus I order twenty dogs and one horse slaughtered for them. They hold a great feast in our honor. This is a strange place. Altomara states she must prepare to give her offering of blood to the Moon Goddess. The moon is full. She enters a long structure of stone covered with earth some half a chain [33 feet] long and several rods [rod = 16.5 feet] wide. A channel brings water from a spring up hill to the rear. The Spaniard states he will stay with her, but she kicks him out. There are many women here all for this purpose. They will stay seven suns. There are several more of these places and we take refuge in them.

The horses are restless. The storm is fast approaching. These people have a person of age who dances around with the necklace of bear teeth and claws around his neck and many feathers in bands about the legs and arms. He also has silver bracelets on and rings in his nose and ears and one through his lip. He has something about his person that rattles as he moves, and he blows a whistle of willow wood. He also has a grotesque mask on a stick and much as a yester [Jackson: "There is no 'j' in Theban thus I believe this to be Jester."] *puts it into faces of others. Tamo states he is chasing away bad spirits which is what the jester would do. The practices are not that different. He is called the Shay-Man or Shaw-Man and is considered a healer and religious leader among his people.*

He tells the children a story. As I understand it once there were no people on the earth and the animals had to decide if they wanted light or dark all the time. The bear wanted dark. A small ground animal wanted light and so did the deer. Others wanted both. Those that wanted light did a dance and it started to get light. At this the bear ran after the little animal, the leader of the group and it ran down a hole but not before the bear's claw raked its back. In the meantime, the animals that wanted both did a dance and the Great Spirit, this I suppose is God, chose half-light and half dark but the little animal to this day has a dark stripe down its back. [Jackson: "I think this describes a chipmunk."] *The children are pleased with this story. Lionel states it is just a story for children, but Wasabee looks at him and states. "Is it?" He looks mollified. I am a second son, but his place is a third son and is worse off than I. As I see him now, I realize that Wasabee has tamed the animal within and am pleased for him. I ask Wasabee if she will go with Altomara, but she states that she has no gift for the Moon Goddess. The storm rages without. Trees are uprooted. A horse is killed. It will be consumed as well. Nothing goes to waste here.*

After the storm and the next morning, I have a chance to look around this place. There are about five hundred persons here some are with men and of the north who live here also and have families here. These people have a custom strange to us. All things have a separate Spirit to them, and each must be kept in balance with all the rest. They tell this story to explain. Once the ground shook and a spring came up. The underworld Spirit gave freedom to the water Spirit. It ran from the north to west and then east till it dropped into another hole but soon emerged again from a split in the rocks at the base of the hill. The people went into this split in the rocks following the course of the water and found a silvery rock. The north people made of wood and hide a device to make fire hotter from below as does the Hammersmith. [Jackson: "Bellows"] *There is a black rock here and it is hard to light but burns very hot when put on a stone pile with the device of the Hammersmith below.* [Jackson: "Coal?"] *A large caldron with this silvery rock broken up and water in it is cooked and what rises is removed. A place in hard clay is cut or in rock in a snake or round pattern and the residue of the caldron is run in it. When it is cold it is worked with stone and bone. The silver ornaments are made thus, and these people would give us half a hundred weight for the Ass. We took it and divided it up among us. That Spaniard gave all his to Altomara and this they are held in higher regard by the people.*

Where the spring came from the earth the people made a stone hut covered with earth as the Sun Spirit was angry with the Water Spirit for showing the people the silver metal and was out strong and held back the rain and the water dried up. To protect it the stone hut was built over it and the stream that ran a chain to the hole of the silver cave was covered in stone and a wall half my height built over it to protect the water from the wrath of the Sun Spirit. This wall serves no other purpose. This is not of good and sound mind. The children use sticks to annoy the ass and it bellows and kicks and this they find most amusing. We are glad to be rid of it.

When the seven days are over the women come out and with them, they bring their blood, and it is given in a ceremony to the Moon Goddess. There is on the hilltop a small circle of three rods across and in it two uprights and a cross piece all of stone. This resembles the Greek letter pi. When the moon is not seen the blood is poured into the circle by the Priestess. This has to my knowledge no effect on anything except the area smells bad always. Not much grows here but one plant that it is stated the roots in a strong drink made of honey will win a woman for a man. This sounds to me as the tale concerning the Mandrake root back home, but I am silent. It does no good to argue with our guest and it is much safer too. The Spaniard states he will try it on Altomara that causes Lionel to ask why. She is already yours he says and that ends that idea.

We have been a fortnight [two weeks] *and are given a strip of hide with tortoise claws and shells long and shiny and said to come from far to the south in the waters of the great sea sewn onto it.* [Jackson: "Dentalium Shells?"] *It will be a mark of protection of these people on us and we will pass through the land of others called the Pea-coot. They will honor the passage and we again return on course.*

A wattle wall surrounds it and around this a high palisade of wood some half a chain in height and pointed at the top. A heavy gate laden with flat stones was barred from within and there were sentry posts upon raised mud and stone platforms within. There were windowed rooms with fireplaces some ten in all with a central chimney to all and a central hall with a banquet table of oak and wood benches about it. As we entered the smell of cooking meat assailed us. A woman called Gianna plays an instrument making a tinkling sound and a clapping sound alternatively. It is an elongated piece of wood tear shaped with two metal thin plates across the width on swivel rods. A drum and horn also accompany her. It is not unpleasing to the ear. I am told it is called a cistrum. To the back was a doorway and a way down to a large chamber but if constructed or natural I could not tell. Many candles provided light while only rustlits did so above. [Dr. Jackson: "Rushlights."] *To the rear on the wall was an effigy of the Goddess with much flowers about her and pine sprigs over her and a well of water before her and lamps of oil about her. To the left was the sign of Blodeuwedd and Cymidei Cymeinfoll with her cauldron of Regeneration the three spirals circling the dot ever present. Also, was the sign of Gwyn ap Greidiawl Creiddlad Gwyn ap Nudd. about the sacred triangle and to the right the sign of Arianhrod.*

There are about forty soldiers here under the command of Darius but some one hundred and fifty are stationed in the valley below though we saw no signs of them upon our advance. In the Temple area the women rule but within the enclosure of the valley it is a mutual rule with Ishtar and Goveneor and Gwyn his partner. There is no king or ruling class, and all agree on what should be done by equal votes both men and women. I find this strange. I am told this is a spiritual place and the body of the community resides to the west many days' journey upon a great lake where they dig and process the copper metal. Some is traded with the local people, but most is traded with the north men. This has been the way of things for hundreds of years I am told.

"Upon the floor of the cavern of the Goddess was a circle of holes around the altar which from five of these holes' lines extended to seven

more holes in a semicircle before a square stone upon which sat a clay cauldron with the spirals on it. The seven holes formed a small semicircle much in the shape of a smile. A woman with a circle of entwined vines about her head and in a white garment of some kind of leather spoke to Altomara: "Are you a virgin of the Goddess?" Altomara went upon her knees and with outstretched arms spoke in language I could not follow ending with Ga-Sto [Jackson: "I am."] The woman then addressed me stating she was called Gywn Mother Goddess of the Temple. Lionel translates. She explained that the holes on the floor represented days of the year. Where the five were was a letter "N" for the Nones of the month and it was of this part of the year that as the five lines showed they came together at the third hole which was of the bright star of the Borialis symbol of Arianrhod. When a wooden peg with a carving of a phallus on it was in the that hole there would be a great festival.

The Spaniard did say unto Altomara that she lied for she was not a Virgin, but she stated that she was for virginity is rather a state of mind than physical condition brought about by the lack of sexual contact. She was a free woman complete unto herself and without any ties to a man that she did not wish to have. This is in fact the basic form of the worship of the Goddess and though it is foreign to me as is the belief of the Prophet of Islam I can understand both from having now read one of the scrolls of Adoniram. I expressed a fervent desire to know more of them and stated this unto Gywn. Thus, I was told I must prepare.

I was taken from the Temple structure and led by a winding path down the side of a mountain opposite that from which we arrived to an overhang of rock blocked up on all sides to its top with a small opening at one end. I was told to spend the night here after bathing in the stream to its left and to which a fall of water preceded from above. On the morrow she would come and get me. I was to eat nothing and to drink no wine. This I thought a yoke [Jackson: "I believe this to be "joke."] as we had no wine since we left Braich Y Pwill in Gwynedd.

Upon the rising of the moon however, she came to me and with a light of an oil lamp the oil of the rendered fat of the goose she stated as the lady of the Silver Wheel descends to earth to watch over the tides of the sea and the tides of human fertility so does her maiden come to me. I told her I had taken a vow of celibacy that I could not break as it was before my God and of this, she seemed pleased. I have tested you and have not found you wanting. She speaks in the language of my land, of Engeolnde [England] much to my surprise. She states she knows many languages and is gone.

On the morrow she returns clothed again in garments and shows me a winding path to the right that leads through a small opening in the rock as one would enter a vagina through a long passage that represents the womb into a large chamber and via a small opening at the back into the light of day in an alcove surrounded by rock. Following a narrow path to a small cave we enter here, and she states I must leave within the sand here an offering. She leaves a likeness of the Goddess Blodeuwedd and I leave some trinkets I have carried with me from home.

She lights two lamps and by them I see that others have left things here also. At the very rear, she states I am to reach into a hole and remove what I feel. It is an uneasy feeling to place your hand into a hole that you cannot know what is inside, but I do so and remove four long clay tubes as were seen by me at the Temple. Within are four rolled scrolls. I will return them to the Grand Master as I was so instructed and for which I was to be rewarded. It is the purpose of my venture here. We leave the way we have come. She states to me that as I have received knowledge from my parents at birth so have I received knowledge now. But as to the birth knowledge it must be learned how to unlock it and this is acquired knowledge. So now as I exit from the vaginal opening symbolic of rebirth so I must wash in a pool for a baby is washed at birth and then climb a set of stone steps to the top of a great rock set in the stream of the pool and sit at its top in a depression there with the carving of the goose at my feet to let the noon sun bath me with its warmth.

She also states that of the four tubes I may choose one as my own. Looking at them I see that each has cut into the clay a letter of the Greeks and I see Alpha, Beta, Eta, Omicron and being anew I choose Alpha. She states that I have chosen wisely. Now I must pass through a long dark corridor between two rocks that has been covered with stone and earth to signify my passage from birth into knowledge. She states I must now spend a night in a different cave opposite the one I spent last night in. On its roof are strange symbols and lines. She states they are *rivers showing the way to their brethren far to the south. There are called the Man-Den, [Mandan Indians?] Cone, Navasak. She also states that Altomara shall not return with us. The Goddess has called her name. She has seen the owl. But of this I do not understand until later."*

When I was alone in the small cave, I set about making a light and by it examined the tube I had chosen. The others were held by Gwyn. In it were four documents. A map on parchment and singed Tantin d Mandrakis. [Jackson: "At the "d" there is a hole in the paper, and I believe the missing letter may an "a" but am uncertain."] *The second document was in Theban and said nothing till I used the discs and then it told of a vast treasure in gold and gems and precious relics including parts of the tablets given by Moses from God and held in a golden chest feared taken by the Romans when they overran Jerusalem and it was hidden below in the tunnels cut for water in the ruined city of Petra in the Valley of Edom and in a cavern with the mark of the crescent moon upon the mountain of Jebel Madhbah. The third document also encoded was of a journey of the Spirit and told of the True teachings of our Lord who came to reveal rather than redeem. Also, of a Seal of Herod to an agreement of union between one Hasmonian princess, Myrian of Migdal and Yeshua ben Yosef* [Jesus, son of Joseph] *of the Royal House of David at Cana."*

When I emerged from the cave the next morning Cedric who had taken Benedictine cowl at Shewsbury admonished me for my actions reminding me of my vows to Our Lady and the Holy Father. I in turn felt the need to respond in kind and did thus remind him of the vow he took with us at the Temple so stating that what I do now is by the order of the Temple and for the Glory of God. If he came upon this quest with other intentions, then his venture has been in vain, and he was silent. However, I know that should by the Grace of God he returns from whence he came that his tongue will be well oiled.

Gwyn has stated that on the morrow is a meeting with the local group at a great rock set on the banks of a river at the base of the mountain by a bald. Both she and Altomara want to meet a man called the Sac Man or Quicksa-Piet. A great healer among the local people called Le Nee Lan-ap-pee which I am told means First People. This mountain we are on is sacred to them as they believe their Great God lives on it but upon the opposite mountain lives the Pan-si-kee a trick player and I think a form of devilish demon. This may prove to be informative.

Clyphus, The Spaniard, Altomara, Lionel, Sir Eldric and I went with Gwyn down the steep slope of the mountain on the side where the caves were the next morning. As we approached the bottom of the ravine through which a river ran, we could see to our right a bald and a large rock set beside the stream. It had a particular shape and reminded me of a gravestone.

To its left was a spire of rock, gray in color spersed with white and the top rounded by man to resemble a phallus. To the right was a rounded large rock that was split through its center. Gwyn stated that on the first day of the third month the sun's rays cast a shadow at midday upon the phallus which then entered the split in the rock to the right towards eventide symbolizing impregnation and marking the next day of festival of the Goddess. [Dr. Jackson: "The months of the year I believe are counted from spring to the equinox. Thus, this event described are counted was about June 21st or close enough to be the mark of Mid Summer's Eve which also coincides with John the Baptist's birth date as set by the Roman Catholic Church."]

Within the left side of the great stone and about the Phallus stone at the edge of the bald were several striking persons one of which was dressed in the hide of a bear with the head and skull of it over his own. He carried a short stick with two shells of a tortoise joined together at the top which he periodically shook making a rattle noise. He had a metal ring through his nose and one through his right ear which looked like silver. He appeared very old, and Gwyn identified him as the Quicksa Pict we were there to meet. The others were dressed in skins and furs with the feathers in their heads and painted up in red and white one in red and black. They were the escort. We approached over a tree set across the stream which had the top flattened to make walking easier. Thunder rolled in the distance, and it was a cool morning.

Clyphus was looking to his left and staring into the forest beyond when I, taking up the rear and in full armor came to him asking what he was looking at. Something is a stir in the forest me thinks he replied.

An animal no doubt I stated but he said, "Nay" and just at that point Altomara was seen making hand signs to the Quicks-Piet with her back to the wood. She pitched forward and the Spaniard cried in a loud voice. Lionel, Gwyn, and Sir Eldric covered the Quicksa-Piet and his people with their shields and drew weapons. I saw that there were feathers sticking out of Altomara's back. Instantly, the Spaniard dove into the woods screaming and flailing his great axe. I was hit with several arrows but only one penetrated the armor and struck flesh in my left shoulder. It was a bolt of a cross bow, and I felt the steel point hit bone. Still, I stood but going to one knee rested a moment before charging after Clyphus and the Spaniard. He had no armor but his mail over a gambeson and some furs yet all of the arrows hitting him in the chest didn't strike home.

He was among the attackers in a short time rushing up hill and the first three went down, one his head rolling down hill and the other an arm missing, the third was cleaved from skull to waist and the axe stuck. Then drawing blade and dagger he charged on. Clyphus dropped two as a third jumped from a rock upon his back, but Gianna of Gwyn's people hit him with his dagger. Sir Eldric now entered the scene, and he too was struck with an arrow in the side between his breast plate and the waist guard, but it was a stone point and turned on his mail. The attacker was sliced both bow and man across the middle and left with his guts spilling out over the earth. Another attacker jumped on Lionel's back, but Wasabee defended her man and cut him across the throat burying her dagger of flint in it. The Spaniard had reached a man pulling something and bending over to do so and was relieved of his head. Thus, Ponce recovered the missing cross bow. The head of this one was presented to Quicksa-Piet by the Spaniard on his knees. I had dispatched several and taken one as a prisoner. The attack was over.

The Spaniard having presented the head which was taken and thrown to the warriors, and they began to kick it around among themselves, then went to Altomara. She spoke to him in a whisper and kissing him she passed to the Goddess. He turned to me and said, "She stated she had seen the owl. The Goddess had called her home.

I will honor her as she wished." The attackers were enemies of the Quicksa-Piet and his people and of the people of the Goddess. They are known as the Cat-skins [Catskills?] and the Sac-Man stated that because of their actions in making war in a sacred place all other groups will not befriend them. Only the five groups of the many fingered rivers to the west [Fingers Lakes of Upstate New York?] would be friends to them. For our actions on his people's behalf there would be peace between his people and those on the mountain for as long as the trees grow, the four winds blow and the sun shines.

Altomara was taken and wrapped in a mat and placed upon the top of the stone tunnel upon a great pile of oak wood of the pine tree and a fire set below her and she was consumed. The bones were gathered and placed in a special box of oak wood and Ponce took her ash and placed it in the jar he carried Myrrh that he had used to wash her body with. Gwyn had her placed in the cave with the carving atop its roof, both ash and bone box and each of us left a grave good. Gwyn left the three scrolls and I the disks but the scroll of Alpha I took with me and later secreted the Eta one also.

Talismans [objects thought to have power to bring good luck] were set upon the cave and Clyphus and Sir Eldric pushed a great rock from above to block the entrance and then we made upon the hide of a deer a chart with the sky tool to mark the place where she was and to mark the place of the [navigation] disks for I knew that Hubert held the others. If the Goddess Priestess thought we could not read the scrolls she may let us have more. It was a good thought as Gwyn had Sir Eldric and Lionel also choose scrolls. We laid out marks on the rocks [Theban letters near Table Rock] so that the chart would be better followed in the future. Clyphus had a chart of the stars for Belt-ane at Cypress, and he felt he could track a course home by making one of the stars here. A large natural stone formation on the side of the mountain of the Goddess suggests a human face in its shape and at the right of this is a ledge that allows one to stand with a complete view of the south, east and north. So, did Clyphus prove of some worth after all. Clyphus did however choose to check his measure-ments upon the morrow at eventide and as he was at work did a rain begin and he cried, "Oh Astroth" and upon this utterance did a lightning bolt strike his metal and he was killed as the rain turned to snow. Gwyn claims it is an omen, but I believe it to be an accident of timely proportions. Now only those of the Templars know the disks are within with Altomara's ash. He is also laid to rest in a cave upon the top of the mountain near the living structure of the Goddess.

I have been laid out in a hut of sticks bent over round and covered with hides. A fire is within, and some evil smelling dried plant is placed in it. The smoke is overpowering, and I become dizzy as though drunk with too much wine. Then I remember nothing. When I awake the arrow is removed and a poultice of the sap of a wide leaf plant covered with the inside bark of a tree and then a leather cuff strapped with lacing about my arm and shoulder has been applied. It is changed four times a day and heals well. The Quicksa-Piet tends my wound himself with a woman called Gerillius of the Temple who is learning this method of healing from him.

With a course set we prepared to depart. Gwyn gave us the blessing of the Goddess and of Arianrhod, Mother of Dylan and Lleu Llaw Gyffes, sister of Gwydion, Niece of Math ap Mathonwy daughter of Beli wife of Nwyvre ruler of Caer SIdi and Caer Arianrhod. More substantial she provided us with a guide as did the Quicksa-Piet of the Len-ap-pe who would guide us to the valley of the Cone for it was in the mind of Lionel that he and Wasabee should reside with them if they would grant them succor [to give assistance or aid] as it was now evident that Wasabee was with child. Lionel did put in my care the scrolls given him and stated that he now had all he ever wanted and with the birth if all went well, he would seek the People of the Goddess to the south that Gwyn called the Man-Den so that Wasabee could be with people she could speak with in her native tongue. It would be his gift to her for the child. I have agreed to release him from his vow, and we set out on thus.

It is very cold, and snow has fallen but the guides Sif and Dane of the Goddess know the way well. From a mountain top we can see far to the west the land of the many rivers as the disconnected fingers of a hand lives the enemies of the Len-ap-pee. We arrive in two days at a sheltered cave near a waterfall on the bank of a large river to the west of the Tall Mountain with water at the top and for the first time meet one of the Co-Han. They look to me as the Ivri. They wear a small hat of woven grasses upon the top of their heads [Yamulka?] and unlike the natives of this place all have much facial hair and long beards. They are of a darker color than those of the Goddess but lighter than those of the native peoples. They have heard of our exploits with Len-ap-pee and the death of Altomara. We are made welcome. Lionel is to be made a member of their group and will be given a place of honor in the Circle. I am happy for him.

Sif tells us we must leave when the snow melts a little and before the river ices up. We will go by water most of the way but must take the boats around a great cataract four days' travel south and then we will reach a greater river. We will wait there till it freezes over and walk to the other side. Then we will travel overland half north to east following the ridges descending all the while till we make a sharp change and go south. We reach a high bluff overlooking another greater river with a small island upon its far shore. Here the river narrows, and it is here we will cross. We begin to fell trees for rafts and are soon upon the far shore. This river is of salt. We pass in three days several stone and earth covered structures but don't stay in them. They are for the women. We cross another river with the help of the local people and to this to an island of great size and travel in a sheltered water way by great bark boats along this to where we can await the thaw to build a boat and sail east to our homeland across the great ocean."

It is strange these people set great importance upon such little things as beads of color which we give them many. As Sif has said it has been accomplished and our year is completed upon the banks of the Great Salt River at the Island of the Man-ap-tl-en peoples. Our escort has left us two days ago at a stone shelter covered with earth and have returned with Dane, but Sif has found it good to stay with us. Ship building will commence soon. I have asked the Spaniard about when he charged up the hill the day Altomara died. He wore no armor but mail, yet the arrows did not stick into his flesh. He cannot explain this except to say that Altomara had given him a copper disk some hand and half round with the symbol of the Goddess on it and wore it on a cord under his coat. It was swinging back and forth so it may have stopped the arrows, but he is not sure. He shows it to me, and it has several dents where points may have struck. I think however it occurred it was a miracle and a result of the Grace of God, and he agrees.

The ship is in the style of the North men [Norwegian Vikings?] but with the sail lateen as has been constructed by Ism'il al-Mutamid who has accepted the Cross of Christ and taken the vows of the Order and is related to Hugh De Payens by the union of his ancestors Abdullah al-Kamal and Zohra. It is of one mast and spar and of only one deck with a portion for some shelter of the stores. We take on skins of water a plant called mace [Jackson: "Maize?"] dried and ground. It is filling food with a little water. Some dried meats and fruits also are provided and when Sif tells us the winds are favorable, we will set her to sail and will make land in two moons and half another by the Grace of God and the Goddess Arianrhod of whom Sif is a Priestess. She will go to the King of the North to tell him of the passing of Altomara and so will the Spaniard go with her as does Ishma'il and Gretchen.

We have finished the oars and they are in place. The ship rides high in the water, and we add ballast of stone. We take it into the sheltered bay with six small islands but stay in the deep channel as there are shoals here. We must practice much with a small crew till we are satisfied that it handles well for us. This island forms two fingers with a bay between and upon the left most point we land, and Sif marks a stone by the stars as to where the Temple lies. Eldric makes a chart and calls this place aligning place as it points both west to the Temple and east towards home. Now we set sail and go with the scrolls to the Temple at Castrum Sepulchri.

..orm [Jackson: "I believe this to be storm"] and the mast is damaged and lower spar cracked but the sail is not damaged. We are all wet and except for Cedric who was aloft all are safe. He has gone to God. May he be received well. God has certainly protected the location of the Temple of the Goddess and the disks as now the Holy Father can hear of it only from one of the Order of the Knights Templar. We are now XII [twelve people] without the Spaniard and Sif. He may return with her to the Temple as his love for Altomara warrants it. I have released him from his vow. Sir Eldric sights land

and we are soon upon a rocky shore, but the hull is undamaged. It is an island on the XL [Forty degrees latitude?] *course.*

We make landfall at Eris Head in two days and three days hence we are at Gwynedd and make for Merthry Tydfil. I have thus returned to the Cistercian Abbey at Castrum Sepulchri in three moons. My shoulder has healed well but pains me a bit when the damp sets in. Father Abslem has sent us brother Antoninus to take down my story so that it can be added to the record by order of the Grand Master, Odon de St. Amand. He has informed me that the map and instructions to the treasure of the Alpha scroll shall be my reward for the valuable service I have provided and having received the Sacraments and been given Absolution I shall be given a command of the Garrison at Petra. This is more than I could hope for.

We have returned with the nine tubes many having several scrolls within, but the marriage document master Odon state is valued beyond measure. Unfortunately, Hubert and his ship was lost at sea thus no discs [used for deciphering scrolls] *remain. A quest is to be assembled to recover the ones with Altomara de Leon, but I shall not be a party to it nor shall Ponce, he hated that name and always wanted to be called the Spaniard. However, the new Grand Master, Arnould de Torogo decides to delay it. I state that all of the above is as I remember it and to so place my sign and name below to so attest this by the Grace of God in the Year of our Lord 1180. (MCLXXX) Ralp De Sedley.*

There is a lot to unpack from De Sudeley's deposition, which both Don and I have addressed in our previous books: *The Scrolls of Onteora: The Cremona Document*, and *Cryptic Code of the Templars in America: Origins of the Hooked X*™. For the Oak Island chapter of this immensely complicated, 800-year history of the Knights Templar's activities in North America to make sense, an overall summary of events will be helpful. Again, for those who are more skeptical about this controversial history our previous books are a must.

THE JACKSON / MARCINKUS CONNECTION

Bill purchased what he and his colleagues called the De Leon File in 1971 from Gustave Benvenuto, in Rome. It was a compendium of encrypted reports, letters, and maps that Don and I later came to call "The Cremona Document."

Bill, Don, and other company colleagues had investigated various aspects of the stories from the document over the years, and traveled to places like Nova Scotia, Newfoundland, Hunter Mountain, the Adirondack Mountains, New Hampshire, North Carolina, and Jerusalem in pursuit of the truth about the stories the document told. By 1994, both the company they worked for and Bill Jackson's investigations into the Cremona Document had come to an end. That year, their company was dissolved, and Bill allegedly sold the document to Archbishop Paul Marcinkus, a Vatican agent who happened to be intimately involved in the death of Pope John Paul I.

Many believe Marcinkus murdered the Pope, as it was rumored the Archbishop had a the key to a secret entrance to the Pope's bed chamber, where he was found dead in 1978. I'm sure it's not lost on the reader that Bill's name in the Yallop book (see photo next page) adds credence to the story that Bill did indeed sell the Cremona Document to Marcinkus in 1994.

Sometime after 1994, Bill Jackson wrote a lengthy, insightful commentary about his experiences with the Cremona Document material that was found on a floppy disc with De Sudeley's deposition already decrypted and translated into English, presumably by Dr. Jackson.

Upon learning about the sale of the document to such a notorious figure, both Don and I were horrified but understood the document had great value, especially to the Church.

In 2017 Don received a package from Bill Jackson's daughter, Melissa, which contained vitally important information and a startling revelation: two original, handwritten maps. Both appeared to have been drawn in the same hand as the four maps Bill sold to Marcinkus, which we had only seen pictures of. Melissa included a copy of a letter written by her father that helped put things into perspective as to what he had actually done with the most important parts of the document.

In addition to the two original maps, there was a third original document filled with Theban letters on both sides that included a crude map of the South Wall of the Temple in Jerusalem. We later figured out it was the first page of the document Bill sold—which in his typed narrative he'd led people to believe was missing when he bought it. This turned out to

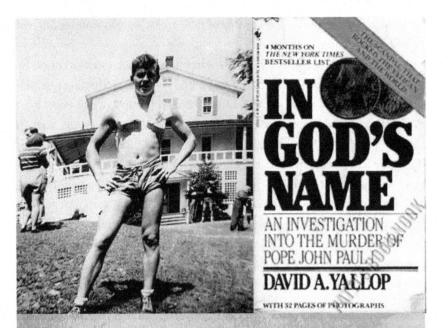

Annaloa Copps, Rupert Cornwall, Monsignor Ausilio Da Rif, Dr Guiseppe Da Ros, Maurizio De Luca, Danielle Doglio, Monsignor Mafeo Ducoli, Father François Evain, Cardinal Pericle Felici, Father Mario Ferrarese, Professor Luigi Fontana, Mario di Francesco, Dr Carlo Frizziero, Professor Piero Fucci, Father Giovanni Gennari, Monsignor Mario Ghizzo, Father Carlo Gonzalez, Father Andrew Greeley, Diane Hall, Doctor John Henry, Father Thomas Hunt, William Jackson, John J. Kenney, Peter Lemos, Dr David Levison, Father Diego Lorenzi, Edoardo Luciani, William Lynch, Ann McDiarmid, Father John Magee,

William Jackson when he was 26 years old in 1966. The name William Jackson appears in the Preface on page 16 of David Yallop's book and given Jackson's known involvement with the P2 scandal this very likely is our William "Bill" Jackson. (Courtesy of Donald Ruh/Internet)

be inaccurate. The truth is, the reason he removed this page was because he didn't want Marcinkus and the Church to have it, as it contained the cipher phrase that was necessary to decode De Sudeley's deposition. We were stunned and relieved to realize that without this page and the cipher phrase, Bill had essentially sold the Vatican a worthless document. Within minutes of studying the two maps, we realized they marked the locations where the Templars had hidden some of their treasures. No wonder Bill had pulled these two maps out.

Another interesting Bill Jackson/Marcinkus connection was found by my friend and Templar researcher, David Brody. While conducting research into the Vatican banking scandal called P2, and the murder of Pope John Paul I, David read a book about the murder called, *In God's Name*, written by David A. Yallop. Don had mentioned that he and Bill were involved in an assignment by the agency Dr. Jackson worked for, to intentionally set up bad guys associated with the P2 scandal in the late 1970s. In a guest commentary on my blog[11], Don wrote the following about that assignment, *"My only involvement in the operation was to carve the symbols on a swagger stick as directed by Bill Jackson. The redacted portions in the letter are to protect persons involved in the P2 matter that are still living."*[12] The point of all this was to note that Bill's involvement in the P2 scandal, as his name appears in the credits of Yallop's book. Skeptics might argue William Jackson is a

copy 5/9/2017

March 23, 1996

Dear Melissa

Keep these enclosed maps for me. They are from the thing I bought from Italy. Mike Kline had it tested to 1800's so the document is a copy or compilation of material from the 12th century. I think one is in Danish the other is definitely in French. The Danish one is probably the coat of Denmark around where Faro Island is now with what I called Esbjerg in my translation of the document but this map calls it "KINGS CAMP". The other is of Islands as you see but no names. I tried to match shapes to some in my atlas but got meager results. One could be Sandoy and another Rousay but am not sure. Number six might be Prince Edwards Island. I was there with Don. I do not want your mother to get to them or she will throw them out. You know how she is with this stuff. If anything happens to me see that they get to Don Ruh. Thanks.

With all my Love,
Your Father

B Jackson

On May 19, 2017, Donald Ruh shared three previously unknown original documents, two maps and a page with Theban text and a map drawn on the back side, from the Cremona Document. This note, written by Dr. William Jackson to his daughter Melissa, in 1996, explains what he thought they depicted and what his wishes were for the precious items. (2017)

---

11 scottwolteranswers.blogspot.com
12 scottwolteranswers.blogspot.com/2018/12/the-truth-about-oak-island-and-cremona.html

Don Ruh is the only person that took my research seriously and has helped me with it over the years so I include this portion to him but wish to do so after I have departed this earth. Since he is the youngest of the ░░░░ personnel I think he will survive long enough for the current political situation in America to have passed on leaving what I hope will be a more open government with less red tape.

The context as to why Bill Jackson left out the most important parts of the Cremona Document was explained in Bill's own hand in a letter Don pulled from the wooden puzzle box and was repeated in a typed letter written to "Brother" John Lennon and signed by Dr. William Jackson dated October 12, 1994. (Courtesy of Donald Ruh)

common name, but because of his known direct involvement with players involved in P2 it suggests this more than is likely our William Jackson.

SINCLAIR/WEMYSS JOURNALS

In 2016, less than a year before our infamous meeting, when Don shared Melissa Jackson's material she had been given by her father in 1996, I was contacted by a woman who claimed to have the personal journals of Earl Henry Sinclair, the first Earl of Orkney, rumored for centuries to have traveled to the Western Lands in North America in the late fourteenth century. After deleting the first two of three messages she sent thinking she was another delusional true believer, it was the third message that got my attention as it included pictures of pages of the journals and of a lambskin map. I called Diana and made plans to meet with her to see the journals and the map. On September 21, 2016, I and fellow Freemason Matt Cranston traveled to the Mormon Temple in Nauvoo, Illinois, to meet Diana to review the one book and map she brought. I filmed the entire encounter and was impressed with the map and handwritten, linen journal I examined. Because of Diana's checkered past and questionable credibility, the journals and explosive information they contained seemed almost too good to be true. Still, there was too much potentially important historical information contained within the twenty books—thirteen written in Latin, two in Old English and five in modern English—to not take them seriously. This began an intense process of vetting the veracity of the material with a small group of researchers and multiple visits to museums, sites in the field in several states and three countries, and to Masonic libraries to review records.

As of the publishing of this book, everything we have been able to confirm within the journals has been vetted out. Even the lambskin map contains similar information as the multiple maps of Nova Scotia Don received from

Bill Jackson. These documents are separated by time, geography, and individuals that could not have known about the other to possibly conspire to create a hoax. The vast amount and complexity of the material in both sets of documents is simply too vast for a group of people to create, let alone an individual. In chapter eight we also go into details about the corroborating evidence, but a quick list of the shared specific evidence contained within each of the two separate sets of documents include the following:

1. Antonio Zeno
2. Dog Island
3. Newport Tower
4. Father Richards
5. Sacred Numbers
6. The Goddess
7. Hooked X
8. Relic/"Bahumet"

On September 21, 2016, Scott traveled to the Mormon Temple in Nauvoo, Illinois, to examine one of the twenty books comprising the Sinclair/Wemyss journals and a lambskin map allegedly drawn by navigator Antonio Zena dated in Roman numerals to 1395. (Courtesy of Scott Wolter)

SACANDAGA LAKE CRYPTOGRAM

The Sacandaga Lake cryptogram is another important Cremona Document message that ties into the messages that Don received from Bill Jackson's friend Roberta in January and February of 2023. In late April of 2022, Don discovered that one of two wooden wall plaques he received as gift from the wife of his friend and colleague, Dave Rian, after his death in 2016, had something hidden inside of it. Janet and I drove from Minnesota to Don's home in Dover Plains, New York to open it.

Among other items, Don pulled out a small, sealed envelope bulging with something stuffed inside. Upon opening the envelope, Don pulled out a piece of paper that once unfolded revealed a twenty-three-inch-long by twelve-inch-wide table of a grid system with each of the approximately 1,600 cells filled with strange symbols. The symbols in the cryptogram were divided into thirteen parts with a different set of symbols used to number each part. At the top and bottom of the grid table were two curious phrases, "A K CANDLE SAGA", and "ASK A LAND CLAIM." Also written at the top, to the right of the first phrase was a date in Roman numerals, MDCCCXCVIII (1898). We all smiled when I pointed out the "X" in the date was a Hooked X.

It would be the next day before we realized the alphabet of symbols and numbering system was written at the bottom, after the thirteenth part, and then both Don and Janet figured out the cipher phrase needed to decode the message was "Sacandaga Lake." At that point, the week-long work of

The front side of one of two wall plaques Dave Rian's wife gave to Don Ruh after her husband's death in 2016. Don later realized one of the plaques contained something hidden inside. Once opened on May 3, 2022, he found the Sacandaga Lake cryptogram. (Wolter, 2022)

deciphering the message began. Once the thirteen sections were placed in their proper numerical order based on the alphabetic sequence in "Sacanda-ga Lake", a strange but important message unfolded:

MDCCCXCVIII (1898)

I saw the lights again. Could be an ill omen. The right one descend-ed upon my winter lodge and behold there stood the likeness of Amon. He was of common dress and medium height; he had about the eyes shown a light blue. He spake unto me in the tongue of the people. "Can ye understand me?" I replied, "Yea, but thou speaketh not of my native tongue, English." He then spake unto me in English saying, "Our Lord has again need of thee. Take up thy belongings and depart in haste to the river of the Mohawks and ▇▇▇▇▇, by the ▇▇▇▇▇▇▇▇. There seek out a Landsman named Jacob who will put you on a craft to travel west to ▇▇▇▇▇▇▇ and north to ▇▇▇▇▇▇. There seek out a Fuller named, Anson, and he will set you with a guide named Kay. He will ask of thee if you have a land cage, reply, 'Just a k candle saga Kay.'" He will guide you northeast by canoe by ▇▇▇▇▇▇▇ ▇▇▇▇▇▇ to the lake. There he shall depart thee. Then go ye west but climb n[o]t Notch Mountain. Seek out the ancient path and logging road north to ▇▇▇▇▇▇ and the ▇▇▇▇▇▇. Then take ye the cross our Lord sent ye to get from the big island and of its size mark out long by short from the rock ledge. At the hump take only the scroll wrapped in goat skin, leave all else. Find there a craft of bark. Make use of it into the big north lake. Then by the river to the ▇▇▇▇▇ ▇. The old one and your Se'wananama' kit [Algonquin Menominee: Sweet Little Thunder] shall have a guest who shall ask of thee if you have a land cage and you shall replay, 'just a k candle saga.' Thus, will ye know him to give to the goat skin scroll. He shall reward ye and forthwith take his leave. Then I shall return to you both and bless your union at Schaauactoda [Algonquin: Schenectady].

It has come to pass that I now have unto my own two stone of gold ore with which I have stilled Little Thunder. So, I know the lights are of angels, yet all are not of the Lord. Some are of his brother. When I saw the old one and my Little Thunder with her long black hair and a new garment of white deer hide adorned with quill work and her eyes wide, a big smile on her face, it was all I ever needed. The old one and Okta-lonli [Choctaw: Blue Eyes] *embraced me and together we walked to the lodge. So has passed the scroll of the Wars of the Lord from the world of men. Know by the sigel of my ancestors all I write is true. Tala' co* [Gray Eagle] *CLY.*

There are a few important points that relate to the messages from Roberta that have bearing on the Oak Island story. The first point is this message—and all six of the messages received from Roberta—are encrypted in different ways. This was done by the Templar order to protect the sensitive information within them. Second, this message along with two of the Roberta messages, incorporate the letter "K", or the name "Kay", as some type of veiled reference to an important person or being. In short, we believe "Kay" is some type of extra-terrestrial (or "angel") involved in this important work with the long-lost biblical document known as *The Book of the Wars of the Lord.*[13] What is also important to know is there are two parts of *The Book of the Wars of the Lord* within the Cremona document material, that to our knowledge, are the only parts known to exist anywhere in the world.

It seems one of the secrets of *The Book of the Wars of the Lord* is the undeniable mention of extra-terrestrials as we see here, and in the messages to come. This is startling and begs the question as to whether the extraterrestrials had anything to do with the treasures buried on Oak Island and ████. So far, there is no indication that they did.

---

13   The explosively controversial content in *The Book of the Wars of the Lord* and why there is no longer any copy known to exist is discussed in our forthcoming book.

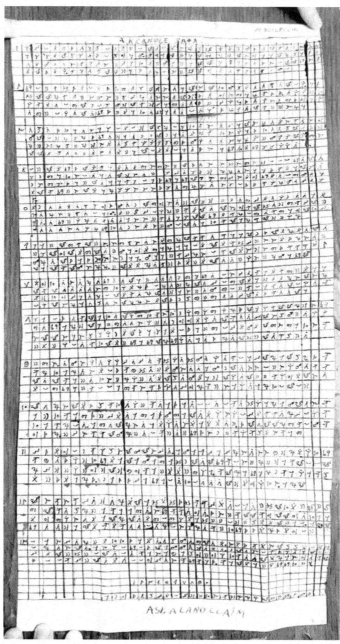

The front of the wooden plaque Don received from Dave Rian's wife contained an Opus 40 brochure, a picture of Dave Rian with friends in 1984, and the roughly 1,600-symbol table of an encrypted message copied by CLY. Don opened the plaque with Scott and Janet Wolter on May 3, 2022.

CHAPTER 3:

THE AUTHORS' HISTORY WITH THE MYSTERY

Coincidentally, both Don and I have had meaningful associations with the Oak Island mystery—most notably in the last several years with the History Channel show, *The Curse of Oak Island*—though, both of us were involved with the mystery years before the hit show premiered in January of 2014.

Don Ruh's experience involved one of his assignments with the private security company he worked with his friend Bill Jackson. Jackson used aspects of the Oak Island treasure story to lure a person to a site where the assignment was completed.

My experience on the island involved a personal tour led by Niven Sinclair, then patriarch of the Sinclair Clan, in August of 2008. He was in Halifax, Nova Scotia, at the invitation of Steve St. Clair to speak at the Atlantic Conference about his work on the Kensington Rune Stone and his then-unfolding research into the Templars in America.

Both stories are interesting and serve as a prelude to what would come next in the vast trove of materials that make up the Cremona Document. A significant portion of which, to our surprise, deals with the extensive activities of the medieval Knights Templar on Oak Island.

The following is my commentary about my experience during the Oak Island tour, why I was interested in the island, and conclusions I drew after the day-long visit.

I was very excited to receive an invitation from Steve St. Clair to speak at a conference in Nova Scotia. I had recently met Steve at the New England Antiquities Research Association (NEARA) annual conference less than a year before. He wanted me to speak about my previously published, scientific work on the Kensington Rune Stone in the book I co-authored with linguist Richard Nielsen titled, *The Kensington Rune Stone: Compelling New Evidence.* At the time, I was immersed in learning everything I could about the interactions between the medieval Knights Templar and the indigenous people they encountered during their more than four centuries of visits to North America prior to colonization. Steve told me he had invited several indigenous people who promised to share stories about their people's interactions with the Templars and I was very excited to meet them and hear what they had to say.

I was also a friend of Niven Sinclair who was co-hosting the conference with Steve, and Niven offered to bring me along on a tour of Oak Island during one of the days we were in Halifax for the conference. I had told both Steve and Niven I was especially interested in examining the so-called "90-foot Stone"—a pillow-sized, glacially rounded stone reportedly found on the island which had carved into it an encrypted message. I had recently coined the term "Archaeopetrography" which is the science I developed that uses laboratory testing and microscopic analysis to determine the relative age of the weathering of man-made images and inscriptions carved into rock. My hope was to try and provide some idea of the age of the carvings in the 90-foot Stone to help with trying to solve the Oak Island mystery.

The conference was well attended, and the speakers were great. I especially enjoyed Ben Olshin and the late Gunnar Thompson's presentations, but it was the lectures given by Michael Thrasher, an elder with the Assiniboin, and Mark and Wendy Phillips, members of the Ojibwe, who shared knowledge of their people's interactions with Europeans long before Columbus. As a story keeper among her people, Wendy explained the tattoos on her arm and the meaning of each symbol. The bear paws represented 400-year intervals of time and how the stories put in her trust dated back to the Ice Age and before. It was riveting to hear her and Mark speak, and I can remember almost everything they said though I won't repeat it as they asked that no one take notes, take pictures, or record the extremely sacred information they shared.

Assiniboin elder Michael Thrasher and Scott Wolter share a laugh at the Atlantic Conference in Halifax, Nova Scotia, Canada, on August 17, 2008 (left). Conference host Steve St. Clair poses for a picture with Wendy Phillips and Niven Sinclair.

They had already heard my lecture before speaking and after they finished it was time to break for lunch. On my way to the cafeteria, I happened upon Wendy who was outside smoking a cigarette and as I walked by, she said to me in quiet voice, "We know all about your people who were here before Columbus." Surprised I tuned to her and said, "You do? How do you know that?" She looked at me, smiled and said, "Because half our people died, they brought plague to us." To say I was taken aback would be an understatement. We chatted for several minutes and then went to lunch. She more than confirmed my speculation about the Templar's and indigenous people's interactions and a few years later I was invited by Mark and Wendy to attend a sweat lodge ceremony in Canada that is still one of the most profound experiences I had in my life. At one point in the sweat, when it was my turn to speak, I said I wanted to ask questions about the Templars. The Medicine man paused and said, "You mean our blood brothers?"

The day after the lectures I traveled to Oak Island with Niven Sinclair, Mark Staveley, Elizabeth Lane, and Matt Sinclair to meet with Dan Blankenship who gave us a lengthy tour of the island. My primary reason for visiting the island was to talk to Dan about the 90-foot Stone. The fabled stone alleged to be roughly 30" long by 16" wide with symbols carved into it comprising an encrypted message that some believe says, "Forty feet below, two million pounds are buried." [14]

---

14   https://www.oakislandmystery.com/the-mystery/inscribed-stone

My thought was to talk to Dan in the hope of locating the inscribed stone and offering assistance with my recently developed scientific method of Archaeopetrography. The success I had with age-dating the Kensington Rune Stone inscription opened the door to examining many other controversial artifacts found in North America. I compared the weathering of the same minerals in tombstones from the Revolutionary War era proving the inscription was centuries old and therefore had to be genuine. Other artifacts I had success with using this newly developed science included the Spirit Pond Rune Stones, the Narragansett Rune Stone, the Bat Creek Stone, and the Tucson Lead Artifacts to name a few. The ramifications of the significant age and therefore authenticity of these controversial artifacts served to rewrite the entire historical narrative of pre-Columbian contact in North America. I felt very confident I could help shed light on the 90-foot Stone inscription, if we could locate it.

Dan was very friendly and took us around the island showing all the well-known locations where various treasure hunters had dug in the past, including the Money Pit and another shaft called 10X. To be completely transparent, I am still a bit confused as to where all the sites are and what each is called that have taken

This picture of the depression of the so-called "Money Pit" on Oak Island shows rotting timbers at the shaft opening and a corroding steel casing once used to protect diggers inside the vertical shaft. (Wolter, 2008)

Matt Sinclair, Mark Staveley, Elizabeth Lane, Niven Sinclair, and Dan Blankenship peer down the shaft known as "10X" inside the building protecting it from the elements. (Wolter, 2008)

The steel casing, ladder, and pipes extending in the shaft known as "10X" were severely corroded as we peered into the hole during our visit to Oak Island in 2008. (Wolter, 2008)

place over the two-plus centuries of digging. However, Dan showed us two sites I recall vividly and took photos of. The first was at the bottom of a large depression with partially collapsed fencing surrounding it. Inside was rotting wooden shoring at the hole and a 4-foot diameter piece of rusted steel casing that at one time was used to keep the Money Pit from collapsing on people like Dan who dug there in the past looking for treasure.

After visiting the famous pits dug in the past, Dan took us into the woods to show us the west side of the island where he said there was strange geomagnetic activity in the ground. Niven claimed it was due to extensive digging underground by cultures dating back thousands of years. When I expressed skepticism, he asked Matt and Mark to break out their copper dowsing rods to see what they might tell us. Both Matt and Mark held the rods in front of them and after a few seconds, first one, then both rods started spinning in a circle. Having played with copper dowsing rods myself before, I watched their hands very carefully knowing that even the slightest movement of their hands could make the rods move. Their hands didn't move at all.

I watched somewhat in disbelief having never seen or heard of dowsing rods spinning, let alone as fast as these were. After a few minutes, I asked if I could try the rods. I held them as I was instructed, keeping them as still as I could. After a few seconds and much to my surprise, the rods began to move, spinning in a similar manner as they had for Matt and Mark. After the puzzling activity of the copper dowsing rods, I concluded the extensive tunnel system below was highly unlikely, but the geomagnetic anomalies in this area of the island was definitely something real even if I couldn't explain it.

After the tour of the island, we returned to Dan's home, and I continued my questions about the 90-foot Stone. Dan understood my interest and what I was hoping to accomplish, but after inquiring throughout the day he was unable to convince me that not only did he not know the whereabouts of the stone, but I concluded there never was a 90-foot Stone to begin with. It was all a myth.

Dan was a complete gentleman and very gracious in spending so much time with us and enduring my questioning him about the 90-foot Stone. As we drove back to Halifax, I thought long and hard about all I had seen and about the enduring question everyone asks who ponders what is the Oak Island mystery: is there still treasure waiting to be discovered somewhere under the island?

Dan Blankenship and Scott Wolter pose for a picture after Dan led a tour of Oak Island. (Wolter, 2008)

My next meaningful interaction with the Oak Island mystery began nearly ten years later in May of 2017. Janet and I first met Don Ruh when we were introduced to him by our friend and fellow researcher Zena Halpern, at a NEARA conference in Newport, Rhode Island in 2006. Don had an artifact he had found in the Catskill Mountains and Zena had recommended I look at it in my materials forensic laboratory to try and help understand the age of the inscription. Two years later in 2008, I was introduced to the Cremona Document material when Don asked if I and other researchers would hike up Hunter Mountain with him looking for carvings and other evidence at a site we now know as the Temple of Goddess.[15]

Zena was with us that day, although she did not join us on the hike up the mountain. In 2010, two years after our hike on Hunter Mountain, Zena and Don signed an agreement to write a book together about the Cremona Document research that was left to Don by the estate of Bill Jackson, in 2004. Bill had purchased the document from a prominent Italian family in Rome

---

15 I have written about that hike and the discoveries we made that day in my book Akhenaten to the Founding Fathers published in 2013.

in 1971 after being led there while researching a mysterious brass, hockey-puck-shaped device hidden inside a decorative ornament Don had found near the shores of Bannerman Island in the Hudson River in 1968.[16]

Zena and Don had made significant headway in their book by late 2013, often asking for my input and testing of multiple inscribed stones and other artifacts found in the Catskills they believed may have been related to the people who lived and visited the Temple of the Goddess in the distant past. Shortly after *The Curse of Oak Island* premiered on History Channel in January of 2014, Zena had become disgruntled with Don and decided to contact the show and share one of the maps from the Cremona Document with them without Don's permission. The map included a two-part depiction of Nova Scotia with parts of Prince Edward Island, the mouth of the St Lawrence River, and the southern part of Newfoundland. Along with lines of both longitude and latitude marked with Roman numerals, the map became a staple on the show as two of the intersecting lines marked a location in Mahone Bay that appeared to be Oak Island.

Over the course of the next couple of years, Don and Zena became estranged as the popularity of the show grew and Zena became a favorite guest—sharing her knowledge of the Cremona material that was used by the show to increase ratings. Zena would eventually publish her own book in clear violation of the agreement she made with Don. I had many conversations with Zena during this time and warned her of the ethical and legal issues ahead as she veered down this dubious path. To be fair, she was a kind and thoughtful woman, but ambition and fame got the best of her and in March of 2017, she published her book, *The Templar Mission to Oak Island and Beyond: Search for Ancient Secrets: The Shocking Revelations of a 12th Century Manuscript.* Because of her appearances on the now-hit show the book did extremely well, and continues to sell as the show is now in its tenth season.

Zena's book was hastily written and filled with inaccuracies and outright fabrications that, had she maintained a professional relationship with Don, could easily have been avoided. Regardless, for fans of the show hungry for a possible connection to the Knights Templar and buried treasure on Oak Island, Zena's book was the raw meat they were looking for. Don of course, was not happy with the events that unfolded, but chose to take the high road

---

16 For a detailed account of the discoveries on Bannerman Island and Bill Jackson's early research into the Cremona Document read Don Ruh's 2017 book, The Scrolls of Onteora: The Cremona Document.

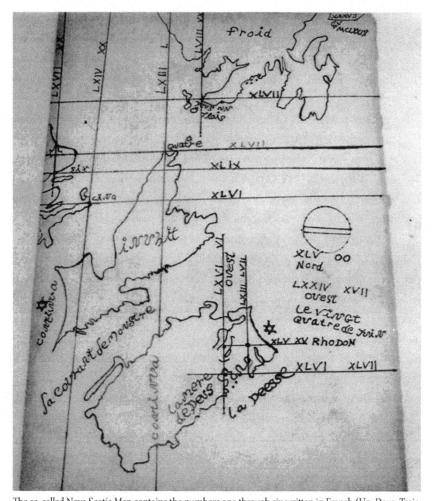

The so-called Nova Scotia Map contains the numbers one through six written in French (Un, Deus, Trois, Quatre, Cinq, Six) that have corresponding lines of latitude and longitude in the upper half of the map. The southwestern half of Nova Scotia has several distinct features that indicate it was added at a later time than the northern part. There is a higher level of detail including rivers, an apparent lake, and islands. The 63° 5 W longitude line (LXIII L) disappears behind the southern half of Nova Scotia indicating a separation from the northern half. Another curious detail is the two Hooked X symbols in the 1179 date and the word "six" on the left side of the map have the hook at the top of the bar as opposed to the Hooked X in the number 45° 00' (XLV 00) just below the circle with two horizontal lines where the hook is below the top of the arm. Could this indicate evolution of the symbol over time? (Courtesy of Donald Ruh)

and ignore the betrayal of his former colleague and friend. I can say with certainty I would not have been as tolerant of Zena's actions if I were in Don's shoes. Sadly, Zena had a relapse of breast cancer during this time and passed away from the disease in May of 2018 at the age of eighty-eight.

As fate would have it, I happened to be traveling and visiting sites on the East Coast and while driving through New York on my way home to Minnesota, I decided to stop and visit Don at his home in Dover Plains. Don filled me in on the latest news about Zena and her newly published book and then showed me a picture taped to his refrigerator. There was Don, standing in the middle, towering over two men on either side of him. I didn't recognize the man on the left but the man on the right I knew instantly was Rick Lagina, one of the two Lagina brothers who star on *The Curse of Oak Island* show! Shocked, I looked at Don and said, "When was Rick Lagina here?" Don smiled and said, "A few weeks ago." He continued, "He came by with his friend Paul Troutman and offered me a contract. Would you mind reading it and give me your opinion?"

He handed me the two-page contract that basically said Don would allow the show to use all of his Cremona Document artifacts, maps, and other documents, pay him nothing, but allow him to appear on the show for his fifteen minutes of fame. After reading the contract, I sarcastically said to Don, "This is great deal Don, you give them permission to use all your stuff, they will make millions in advertising revenue, pay you nothing, and make you famous like Zena by appearing on the show. This is a great deal, I'd sign it right away." Don looked at me for a brief moment and then said, "I'm not signing that damn contract."

Don then changed the subject by handing me a large envelope and said, "Take a look at this. It's a package I received from Melissa Jackson, Bill's daughter." I reached in and pulled out four strange-looking pieces of paper. Two were hand-drawn maps with illustrations on the back of each one that appeared to have been pages ripped from an old book. The third piece of paper was old with what looked like vertically aligned staining on the page that was covered with what I recognized to be Theban symbols on both sides. The back side also had what appeared to be a crude sketch of a map. I was definitely intrigued and then looked at the last sheet of paper that was a short letter written by Bill Jackson to his daughter and dated March 23, 1996. Little did I know at that time, but it was a clue to what would become obvious over the course of the next few years, that Bill had disseminated the most important parts of the Cremona Document. By the time I left, Don and I agreed we wanted to write a book together, or two, and signed an agreement before I left.

Over the course of the past several years, I was invited four separate times to appear on *The Curse of Oak Island* and respectfully declined each time. The first

Don Ruh towers over Paul Troutman and Rick Lagina in a picture taken during their visit in April of 2017. Rick and Paul tried unsuccessfully to get Don to sign a contract giving The Curse of Oak Island show exclusive use of his Cremona Document material. (Courtesy of Donald Ruh)

time I was asked was early in the series when they wanted me to talk about the Hooked X, a symbol that appeared twenty-two times on the Kensington Rune Stone which I had trademarked and written a book on which was published in 2009. I didn't see how the symbol could be plausibly connected to the Oak Island story and I was still busy filming America Unearthed so I declined. Not long after, I was alerted to an episode of the show where Rick Lagina reportedly found a stone he claimed had a Hooked X symbol carved into it. I watched the show and was less than convinced it was a legitimate discovery, much less anything connected to the monotheistic dualism of the Hooked X.

In the summer of 2018 I received a call from the now-late president and creator of Prometheus Entertainment, Kevin Burns. He asked if I would appear on The Curse of Oak Island and I said, "I can't Kevin." He asked, "Why not?" I said, "Because you plant things on the show. I can't be associated with that." He then asked, "What are you talking about?" I explained how the stone with the Hooked X carving was obviously planted and told him that I didn't believe the Lagina Brothers and their crew were the first people to walk the beaches of the island with metal detectors. Kevin responded, "Well we didn't tell people it (the

Hooked X carving) was real." I then said, "But you left the audience with the impression it was real, I'm not coming on the show." Kevin called me again a few weeks later and although our conversations were very cordial and he had a good sense of humor, there was no way I was going to appear on the show, especially after what happened with Zena and her betrayal of Don. Sadly, a couple of years later in 2020, I received news that Kevin had died suddenly at the age of 65.

The other thing that came from our meeting at Don's that day in May of 2017, is I told Don he needed to write a book about his knowledge and experience of everything he could recall from his friend Bill Jackson and the Cremona Document material. Specifically to recall everything he could about he and Bill's discovery of De Sudeley's scuttled ship off the coast of Newfoundland in 1971, and their discovery of Altomara's tomb on Hunter Mountain in 1977, after six years of hiking the Catskills. Don gave me an incredulous look and said, "I don't know how to write a book." I responded, "I'll help you. I'll write an outline of what I think should be in there and you fill in the rest." Don shrugged and said, "Alright..." Roughly a year later, he published his 456-page book on Lulu titled, The Scrolls of Onteora: The Cremona Document.

The next time Oak Island would enter our lives was in the most unexpected way imaginable. On February 21, 2021, the founder of the private security company Don and Bill both worked for, Dan Spartan, passed away at the age of seventy-nine. A couple of weeks later a roughly eighteen-inch square puzzle box arrived at Don's home from Dan's wife. Don called and told me about the box, and I said, "Don't open it! We will be out there in a week or two and we can open it on camera."

On March 4, 2021, with the camera rolling, Don, Janet, and I lifted the lid of the box after Don had cracked the code about how to open it. There were several items connected to the Cremona Document material, but the biggest prize of all was a large paper map we now call Map 8. Later examination would reveal the map had thirteen parts. We also figured out the four maps Bill Jackson had sold to Archbishop Paul Marcinkus in 1994 were included on Map 8 with additional details the maps he sold didn't include. After examining the large paper map, Don found another smaller paper map wrapped in tin foil to protect it in a secret compartment in the bottom of the box. This map we realized was a detailed depiction of Nova Scotia with writing in French at various locations.

My first thought after our initial review of the maps was how skeptics would criticize and attack modern paper maps with historic information. It was at that point our minds went back to the first thing we pulled from the box—a letter written by Dan Spartan. We read it carefully as a smile came to my face. Dan had anticipated criticism and wrote a detailed affidavit explaining how Bill Jackson had given him an animal skin roughly three feet by two feet in size with a separate, smaller map in the neck area of the animal. He wrote how in 2010, the hide smelled and was rotting so he and his teenage son copied the map onto wrapping paper—including a separate piece roughly sixteen inches by twelve inches in size that came from the neck area of the hide. They copied the Nova Scotia map onto that piece which we later named the "Neck Map."

After examining the Neck Map more carefully, we noticed two small islands drawn next to each other in the Mahone Bay area where Oak Island should be. A line was drawn from the islands and labeled in French, "Sept et Neuf." A quick search on Google Translate revealed the numbers, "Seven and nine." We then noticed the same words in French along the bottom of the map. To the right were the words, "Tresor de Depot", with the Roman numerals "MCCCXCV". The English words Google Translate gave us made our jaws drop, "Treasure deposited 1395."

To the right were more French words and another Roman numeral, "Suppime' Même MDCCLXCVIII." The Google translation was confusing but later a friend in France told us the words meant, "Delete same." Just as we had suspected, according to this map there indeed was treasure at Oak Island but had been recovered long ago. The Roman date proved to be somewhat problematic. We could see whoever copied the date struggled with the last few numbers and erased it, eventually settling on a Roman numeral that wasn't correct. We surmised the date was likely 1769 which would eventually be proven correct when the final cache of mind-blowing documents appeared two years later.

It was strange to suddenly have the answer to the centuries-old mystery so unexpectedly appear. The other realization the Neck Map led to was that since the Cremona Document was a record of the Templars' activities—both before and after their suppression by the Church and the King of France in 1307—the existence of the treasure hidden on Oak Island—which was long-suspected but never verified to have been placed there by the medieval Knights Templar—was now proven. What was missing but would soon be

Janet and Scott Wolter, and Donald Ruh open a wooden puzzle box bequeathed to Don from Dan Spartan. Inside the box were numerous items left with Dan by Bill Jackson, including Map 8 and the Neck Map. (Courtesy of Julie Burke)

revealed, were the details about what happened on Oak Island starting in the year 1395 when Earl Henry Sinclair and his eight ships visited the Western Lands bringing not only treasure, but the literal bloodline itself, in over one-hundred Templar knights who would stay behind.

As amazing as the Neck Map and its revelation about Oak Island was, it would turn out to be only a snippet of what was to come. In January of 2023, Don would track down a close friend of Bill Jackson who was now eighty-one years old and had recently suffered a stroke. This person said they had documents Bill had given them, and ended up giving the documents to us in two parts. The first part included a page with an encrypted message in the form of strange symbols on both sides of the page, and a map of what we quickly realized was of the infamous island.

The second trove of material they gave us was comprised of three pages of sketches and four encrypted messages on a total of eighteen pages. In keeping with all the other encrypted messages that make up the bulk of the Cremona Document material, each message was encrypted differently. After two weeks of working together to decode the messages, Don and I were able to finally read the reports and understand the sketches. The messages were nothing short of incredible. Roughly half the material dealt with the details of the activities on Oak Island over a four-century-long period, and they did not disappoint.

My most recent encounter with the Oak Island mystery was somewhat bizarre and happened at the end of October in 2022 when I was part of a historical tour. On October 28, 2022, Tony Sampson, a diver who worked on The Curse of Oak Island show for several years, led our tour group on a twelve-seater pontoon boat to Oak Island sharing stories about the history of the island and his involvement on the show. At one point Tony cut the motor, roughly 75 yards off the northern side of the island, when we noticed a group of people near the shore. Tony said it was the film crew shooting part of an episode for the show when his cell phone rang. He answered and began chatting with the field producer in charge of the shoot. It was a very cordial, short conversation and several seconds after they hung up, Tony's phone rang again, this time on Facetime. Tony answered and then turned the phone toward me and said for me to say hello. Truth be told, I wasn't overly comfortable being on this part of the week-long tour and didn't know what I was supposed to say to this person I had never met on this call. It was a bit awkward, but again very cordial. I wasn't sure what to think, but with the cold wind blowing and chilling us all to the bone, I was glad when Tony turned the boat back to the docks and our soon-to-be warm cars waiting for us.

Looking back on my own history with the Oak Island mystery, I have to say it has been a strange journey that has only gotten stranger with the latest Cremona Document material. I hope those who read this will enjoy the rest of the story.

Tony Sampson, Scott Wolter, and Hayley Ramsey pose for a picture on a pontoon boat off the shore of Oak Island, Nova Scotia, during a guided tour hosted by Scott and Hayley on October 28, 2022.

CHAPTER 4:

ZENA HALPERN AND THE CURSE OF OAK ISLAND SHOW

Don is also open about his personal experience with Zena, her book, and her decision to approach the *Curse of Oak Island* show. In December of 2018, I asked Don to write a guest blog on my website[17] about what happened between him and Zena.[18] His reason for writing this was to ensure the correct, factual information and context was accurately documented for the historical record regarding the Oak Island map, its relationship to the Cremona Document, and the chain of events that led to the confusion about the authenticity of the map. Literally millions of people have already, and continue to watch episodes of the History Channel show that has presented factually incorrect information about these documents. The following is Don's commentary from my blog in 2018, edited for clarity:

> *This blog was written to provide clarity about two documents that have repeatedly been the subject of past episodes and is currently being featured on episodes airing on Season 6 of the History Channel show,* The Curse of Oak Island. *Last season, the late researcher and author, Zena Halpern, presented a map to the Lagina brothers that clearly shows Oak Island along with several words, names, and phrases written in French. Ms. Halpern appeared on the show and explained the map was related to what she called a "Templar Document", but from here on will be referred to as the Cremona Document. The Cremona Document, and the Oak Island map, were the primary subject matter of Ms. Halpern's 2017 book,* The Templar Mission to Oak Island and Beyond: The Search for

17 scottwolteranswers.blogspot.com
18 https://scottwolteranswers.blogspot.com/2018/12/the-truth-about-oak-island-and-cremona.html

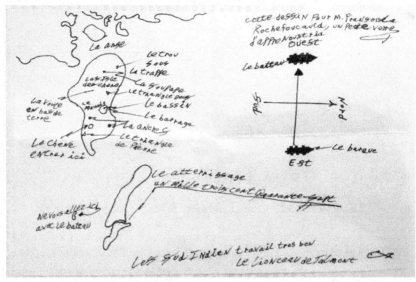

This map, which appears to show Oak Island, in Nova Scotia, was posthumously given to Don by his long-time colleague and life-long friend, Dr. William "Bill" Jackson, in 2015. The French words translated into English are as follows: *Cette dessin pour M. Francois La Rochefoucauld, un petite verre d'apprenoustria* (The drawing for M. Francois Le Rochefoucauld, a small glass/cup of apprenticeship), *Le anse* (The cove), *Le Trou sous La trappe* (The hole under the hatch), *La Soupape* (The valve), *Le triangle dec(e)s* (The death triangle), *Le Bassin* (The basin), *Le Barrage* (The dam), *La Ancres* (The anchors), *Le Triangle de Pierre* (The stone triangle), *Les Isle des Chene* (The isle of oak (Trees), *Le Marois* (The marsh/swamp), *La Voute en bas de Terre* (The vault below ground), *Le Chene entrer ici* (The oak, enter here), *Ne Vous allez ici avec le bateau* (Don't go here with the boat), *Le atterrissage un Mille trois cent quapante-sept* (The landing, 1347) and *Les sud Indian travail tres bon le Lionceau de Talmont* (The south Indians were very good/well. The lion cub of Talmont). (Courtesy of Donald Ruh)

Ancient Secrets: Shocking Revelations of a 12th Century Manuscript. *That 12th Century manuscript is the Cremona Document.*

First, a little history about how the Cremona Document and Oak Island map came into my possession which I then shared with Ms. Halpern. Beginning in 2006, and over the course of the next several years, I inherited several parcels of documents from a work colleague and my lifelong friend, Dr. William "Bill" Jackson. Bill died in 2000 and left the material to me that included the Cremona Document Bill purchased in Rome in 1971, and the Oak Island map he acquired in 1994. In 2008, Bill's estate transferred ownership of all the original documents, and the legal intellectual rights to the material, to me as evidenced by the third page of the agreement signed by Bill's survivors which is seen below.

I first approached Ms. Halpern in 2004 for help with an inscribed stone I found in the Catskill Mountains, and she agreed to do so. Later,

said documents at any time in the future giving Mr. Ruh sole
literary rights to copyright and publish said documents.

This document consists of three printed pages numbered
Page 1.   Page 2.   and Page 3.

[signature: Mark Jackson]   December 10, 2008
Signed   Mark Jackson   Dated

[signature: Pauline Herman]
Witness   22 Bradbury Place Belfast Ireland
[signature: Donald Ruh]   028-9059-1999
Signed Donald Ruh   12-29-2008
       Dated

[signature: Karl Kern]
Witness
[signature: Patricia ...]   9 GRAND ST Bethel Ct 06 8c
Witness
[signature]   12/27/2008
Notary   Dated

Patricia B. Kern
Notary Public, State of New York
No. 01KE6042168
Qualified in Putnam County
Commission Expires May 15, 2010

Page 3 of the legal document transferring all legal rights and ownership of Dr. William Jackson's documents and research into the Cremona Document story, which includes the Cremona Document material and the Oak Island map to me. (Courtesy of Donald Ruh)

she would also work closely with me on the Cremona Document material I inherited. We formed a partnership, and both signed a written agreement in 2009/2010, to write a book about our collective research. A copy of that signed agreement between Ms. Halpern and myself is attached.

In 2015, Ms. Halpern and I had a disagreement related to a person from Los Angeles in the television business Ms. Halpern was in contact with him about doing a story related to our collective Cremona Document research. The disagreement led to a falling out in 2016, at which time Ms. Halpern chose to forge ahead with publishing the book without me. Around that time, she also decided to approach the Lagina Brothers with the intention of sharing the story and appearing on The Curse of Oak Island *show without my involvement or participation. Needless to say, I have not received anything in compensation for the book, or acknowledgement for the content that legally belongs to me which was given by Ms. Halpern to the Lagina Brothers and has since been presented in multiple episodes of* The Curse of Oak Island *program.*

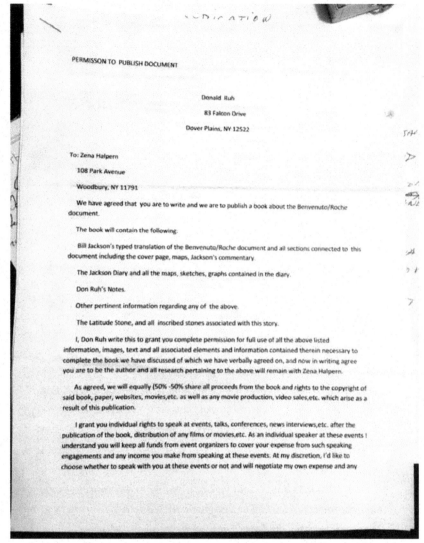

This page and opposite: Both pages of the agreement between Don and Zena Halpern signed in 2009/2010. (Courtesy of Donald Ruh)

What the public needs to know, that Ms. Halpern never knew, was the Oak Island map—which came into my possession in 2015—was NEVER in any way connected to the Cremona Document material or the medieval Knights Templar.[19] The Oak Island map is a fabrication,

19 In light of the most recent trove of messages Don received from Roberta in 2023, it is possible Bill created the Oak Island map using information from the detailed messages and drawings we now know he had in his possession.

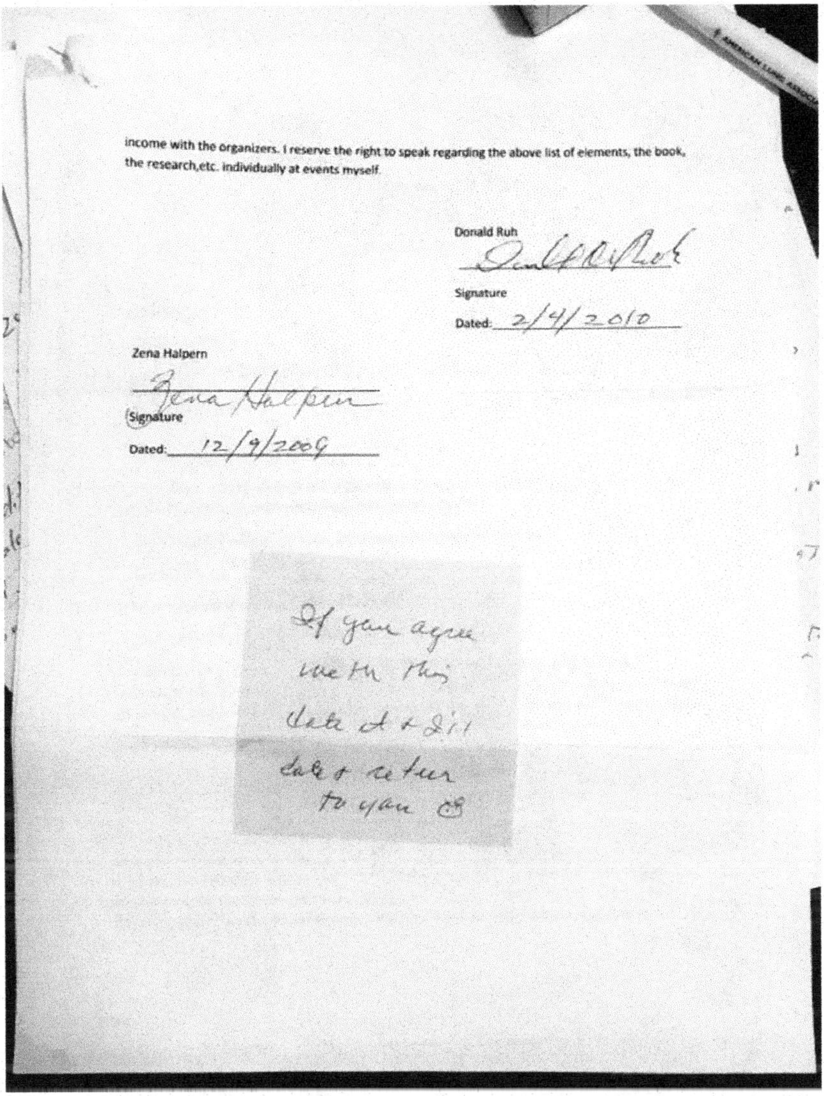

income with the organizers. I reserve the right to speak regarding the above list of elements, the book, the research, etc. individually at events myself.

Donald Ruh

Signature

Dated: 2/9/2010

Zena Halpern

(Signature

Dated: 12/9/2009

*If you agree
with this
date & sign
date & return
to you* ☺

most likely created by Bill Jackson as part of an assignment by the agency Dr. Jackson worked for to intentionally set up a bad guy associated with the P2 scandal in the late 1970's. Shortly after I discovered the Oak Island map—hidden within the pages of a book by Bill in 2015—I showed the map to Ms. Halpern who immediately assumed it was connected to the Cremona Document story. At the time, even I was unclear of the map's association to anything until I recently found

The "…person from Los Angeles in the television business Ms. Halpern was in contact with…", was a man named Chris Finefrock. Scott had been in contact with Mr. Finefrock in 2011 also about a television project that never came to fruition. Don did research into Mr. Finefrock and did not find him credible and chose not to work with him. This greatly disappointed Zena and was just one aspect of the issues that led to their going separate ways.

the letter below in my voluminous records that put the Oak Island map into proper context. My only involvement in the operation was to carve the symbols on a swagger stick as directed by Bill Jackson. The redacted portions in the letter are to protect persons involved in the P2 matter that are still living.

August 21, 1979

Don

Dan and Drake have suggested that I ask you to engrave something for us. We needed to come up with some means to entice the Propaganda Duo people to want to bid on the Ely letter whose back we have imprinted with a design that appears to have a solution to the Oak Island Treasure. Bishop Marcinkus is very interested in this according to members of the ▮▮▮▮▮ Agency. We have decided to use some of ▮▮▮▮▮▮▮s people to hide the letter somewhere. Then we will take the Saint James blade from the swagger stick▮▮▮ acquired from Nash storage and place clues to the letters location on it. I thought long and hard about this and think we can use the location where you and Colonel ▮▮▮ found the ▮▮▮▮▮▮▮▮ stuff at the base of Hunter mountain. I also think I can use the pictures I took from Mr. Roach's home in Wyoming and enhance them with tidbits from the ▮▮▮▮▮ cave location to put the hiding place on Hunter at or near the same location. Dan will get that pot head ▮▮▮ to snitch the idea that the blade has the location engraved on it to the P2 guys. When they go with him to retrieve it we can either follow them to their sources or apprehend them and submit them to ▮▮▮ questioning. Dan needs to have something on the blade that will point to ▮▮▮ so that the implication he is involved in this search, since he has been a great financial supporter of P2 since 1946, and a recipient of one of Delores gifts, will give credence to his participation and alleviate suspicion away from him as ▮▮▮ ▮▮ So I have come up with the following design for inclusion on the blade. You come up with the ▮▮▮▮▮▮▮▮ When you can do this let us know and we will bring the blade to you. We have about a two week window here. Thanks.

Sincerely,

[signature]

The letter written in 1979, by Dr. William Jackson to Don Ruh explained how the Oak Island map was made to create a fictional connection to the Oak Island story to entrap a bad guy who was a Vatican agent involved in the P2 scandal. (Courtesy of Donald Ruh)

Certainly, mistakes were made by the late Ms. Halpern, in part due to her declining health and strong desire to get the story out to the public. However, those mistakes have resulted in false information that has already been presented to the public on television with apparently more to come. This letter is an attempt to set the record straight. The Cremona Document and Oak Island mysteries are complicated and confusing enough and it's important to get the facts straight if there is any chance of getting to the truth about these stories.

I would also appreciate the artifact (The so called "Hebrew Stone")
and all the Cremona Document related material that were in Ms. Halp-
ern's possession at the time of her death, that belongs to me, be returned.
Respectfully submitted,
Donald Ruh

At the time Don wrote this, Zena had recently passed away from breast cancer at the age of eighty-eight and it was only after her death he decided it was time to tell the truth about what happened between them. So much has come forward since the events with Zena happened, that the story on Oak Island has completely changed and we want to be fair to both Zena and the truth about what occurred on the island. We'll wait to go into what we believe is the actual story about the Oak Island map with the comments in French when we share another more detailed map of the island that came forward in early 2023 in Chapter 5, but first a little history about the map.

On page 310 of Don's book, *The Scrolls of Onteora: The Cremona Document,* he wrote that Bill Jackson met with a member of Roachfaucould-Dudonville family, who was likely related to the Roach/Roachfaucould individuals mentioned at various times in the documents. This man was a prominent architect in France who died in 1995. Bill acquired several pages of material from him which included the Oak Island map written in French. This map was later found in a book that belonged to Bill Jackson and we presume he hid it there. The book was titled, *Palestine Before the Hebrews* by Emmanuel Annati, and Jackson gave it to his friend, Mr. Salzano in 1998. When Salzano died in 2016, the executor of the estate gave the book to Don who then loaned it to Zena Halpern. During a visit to Zena's home, Don discovered the last two pages were glued together leaving an opening at the top creating a pocket. Inside the pocket were two items; one was a hand drawn map of what appears to be Oak Island in Nova Scotia, with several lines of text written in French. Zena took possession of the map and shortly thereafter brought it to the Lagina Brothers and the rest—as they say, and pardon the pun—is history...

The second item found in the pocket was a page with symbols that were part of a cipher containing a secret message supposed to be what was carved on the so-called 90-Foot Stone that has magically disappeared. The page had lines drawn through the cipher suggesting it was to be cut up and separated to protect the message. This page is pictured in Don's book and a picture of the decoded cipher message is a few pages later. Don was able to decipher what appears to contain information about the underground workings at Oak Island:

> "Halt no earth cover dig to forty foot with an angle forty five degree, the shaft at five hundred twenty two to you enter the corridor of one thousand sixty five foot reach the chamber."

Besides writing about the two mysterious pages found in the pocket of the Annati book, Don also shared a personal story in his book that shed more light about his interactions with Zena and his colleagues at the private security company he intermittently worked for from 1961-1994:

> On December 13, 2016, I was invited to visit my friend John Drake who was staying in a hotel in Poughkeepsie, New York. I attended a Christmas party of the Lower Hudson Chapter of the New York State Archaeology Association, of which I am a member, at Croton Point Nature Center and then left there to visit my friend in Poughkeepsie, N.Y.
>
> I was pleasantly surprised to find that he had also invited Mr. Joel Harrison of Florida, with his daughter—who had been born deaf, and Mr. Daniel Brandon, Mr. Daniel Spartan, and Mr. Henry Morgan from Portugal, to join him also. It was a big, wonderful surprise to see some of these old friends that I had not seen since 1994. The sad note to the meeting was to learn that Mr. David Rian had passed away earlier in the month and that Joel Harrison had been diagnosed with pancreatic cancer and given six months to live, as of October 2016.
>
> Joel was, however, taking it well. As usual, Mr. Spartan and the others wanted to know when the book I was working on with Ms. Halpern, for the last ten years, was going to be published. Of course, by then I knew that the collaboration had come to an end.
>
> They also brought up reminiscences about Bill Jackson. Joel mentioned that Bill had sent him photographs of seven odd-shaped documents with a request to forward them to Mr. Rian, as the later had moved to a southwestern state and Bill was currently out of touch. Bill wanted the cryptic characters on the pieces to be deciphered. Obviously, they were not just in Theban but were further encrypted

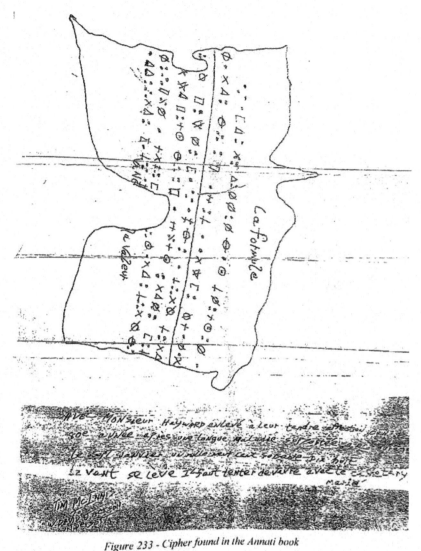

Figure 233 - Cipher found in the Annati book

This page which includes a cipher of symbols with the message allegedly carved on the so-called 90-Foot Stone which has not been proven to exist, about how to access a secret chamber below Oak Island. Below is a message written in French that does not appear to be related to the Oak Island or any of the other Cremona Document material. The difficult to read message is as follows: *Avec Monsieur Hayward en leve' à Leur tendre affection dan seues goe année après une longue maladie supposteé arc covrege le sept Janvier un mille neuf cent sei sante-dix huit [1968] Le vent se lève Ilfaut tenter de vivre avec le cimetary. Merié* (With Mr. Hayward removed from their tender affection in a year after a long-supposed illness arc covered on the seventh of January, one thousand nine hundred and sixty-eight (1968). The wind is rising, we must try to live with the cemetery. Marie). The message was apparently written by a Mr. Tim McGinnis to William David Jackson, who was Bill Jackson's father. (Courtesy of Donald Ruh) *with an unknown key word or phrase. Joel did as requested, but Mr. Rian decided to send the photographs to Mr. Caron in Portugal.*

Since the backs of the pieces had something drawn on them, Bill had photographed both sides of each document. Mr. Caron only wanted the ciphered fronts and that is what he got. Presumably, he sent Bill the translations that I do not have. Joel was left with the backs of the pictures. These eventually found their way into his computer that was using Windows XP. Later Joel printed stuff out so as not to lose them when he transferred to Windows 7. Joel asked me if I wanted the pictures of the backs of these documents, and of course I did.

On January 6, 2017, Joel emailed me the pictures. On January 24, 2017, Joel passed away from a heart attack while he slept. When I saw the odd-shaped documents, I recalled I had seen three of these shapes before. Two came from the pieces of paper in the clay container from the Hudson River during our "fishing trip," outlined in Chapter 2. One came from the page displayed above with the symbols on it. The top line only, was from the stone buried 90 feet down on Oak Island. The remainder I had never seen before, but to my way of thinking resembled pieces of a jigsaw puzzle.

I cut the pieces out and then fitted them together resulting in what appears below. This I shared with Mr. Rick Lagina of the television show, The Curse of Oak Island. *I requested that if it was useful, that he give both Bill Jackson and I credit for the discovery, and he said he would."*

I have a personal side note to share relating to the Zena and Don saga that came from another of Don's closest friends and the founder of the agency he and Bill worked for, Dan Spartan. Once he learned Don and I were working together, Dan and I corresponded for roughly five years starting in 2017, during which time he wrote multiple letters with insight and information related to the Cremona Document. One letter in particular made his feelings known—in no uncertain terms—about what happened between Zena and Don. The letter was written on October 29, 2017.

Besides the obvious disdain Dan Spartan had for how Zena treated Don with her poor decision-making, what is also important to understand is the tight bond Dan had with Don who he had known and worked with since they were both in High School in the late 1950s. I know about the dangerous

Figure 242 - Part Five of 7

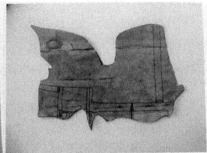

Figure 238 - Part one of 7

Figure 243 - Part Six of 7

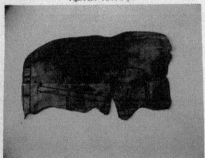

Figure 239 - Part two of 7

Figure 240 - Part Three of 7

Figure 244 - Part Seven of 7

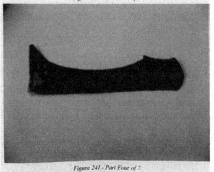

Figure 241 - Part Four of 7

Don Ruh's friend Joel Harrison gave him pictures of a drawing that had been cut into seven pieces showing what appears to be the tunnel system beneath Oak Island. The drawing is reminiscent of two pages of sketches Don received from Bill Jackson's colleague and friend Iudea in February of 2023. (Courtesy of Donald Ruh) work Don, Bill, and Dan performed while working for their private security company, often risking their lives. In my view these guys are heroes for the work they did. That is why I, in a weird way, felt honored to have my life threatened by a man I greatly respected and hoped to one day meet (see letter on following pages). Dan learned of my desire to meet him and sent a beautifully worded letter explaining how we would never meet and how the man named Dan Spartan died the day he retired and moved to Southeast Asia to live out his days. Although disappointed, I understood and respected why Dan had to disappear and took pride in knowing the work I was doing with Don was appreciated.

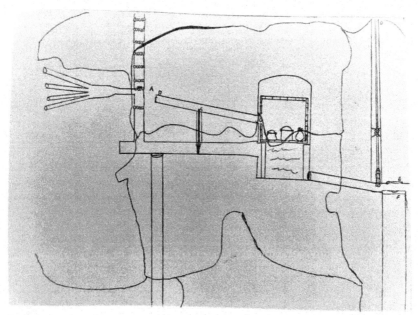

This page shows the seven parts assembled into a sketch of "The Underground Project" beneath Oak Island that is very similar to of two pages of sketches Don received from Bill Jackson's colleague and friend Iudea in February of 2023. (Courtesy of Donald Ruh)

October 29, 2017

Dear Sir

I am not certain when you will receive this package as it is being sent through several Postal Offices both here and in the United States to insure anonymity.

I have been apprized that you are collaborating with my dear friend Donald Ruh on a mutually beneficial project involving William D. Jackson's work. I hope that this will be more in Don's favor than working with the Jewish woman produced. Though I shared material with her in good faith she failed to reciprocate in kind with regards to my friend. That is most unfortunate though we foresaw such an event and withheld certain information pending Don's review of their jointly prepared manuscript which never came about. I hope that will not be the case with you.

I understand that inch and one quarter iron pipe and pipe caps can still be purchased in the U.S.A. A plastic bag with the proper materials within between two such caps, one with a one eighths inch hole drilled in it's center, because iron oxide and such materials could cause spontaneous violent results, with a six to eight inch cannon fuse through the hole could be manufactured by associates of mine in the U. S. This is usually affixed via a strong magnet held to the pipe by magnet wire, which is inexplicably non magnetic, to the undercarriage of a vehicle. The free end of the fuse has about six to eight stick matches epoxied around it and taped with heat resistant tape to the exhaust pipe. This will cause the Minnesota Fire and State investigators WORK trying to identify Mr. Crispy's identity. Not that such a thing would ever be done in reality as that would be highly illegal. Not to mention fatal to the driver.

Never the less the enclosed material has been in my possession since it was sent to me after Mr. Peter Carson died in 2001 and was in his safe having been sent to him by Mr. Jackson some time in the 1980's. The stones and shells etc. were all taken from what Bill Jackson called the Blocked Up Cave. This was located on Hunter Mountain in the Catskill Park between Mr. Bilda's shack and the place where the Native American's erected their Teepee just before passing through the rock cut to get to the Sand Cave Passage. This so called cave was a rock ledge created by sandstone eroding within it to create a hollow space about 6 feet by 4 feet by 7 feet high. Loose stones have been piled with mud between them to form a wall in the front of it about 4 feet high. This wall had a hollow space in it like a fireplace but that was not it's purpose. That was probably ceremonial in nature. Jackson believed it was where the person referred to as Ralp, presumably Ralph de Sudeley, spent one night and the Goddess priestess offered herself to him. I do not think that most of these rocks are native to that area especially the clear crystal ones. As a Geologist you would know better than I however. We thought you might want them and this is the last of Bill Jackson's stuff we have to give away.

This page and opposite: The first of two letters sent to Scott Wolter by Dan Spartan on October 29, 2017. The not so veiled threat was written by Spartan as warning not to take advantage of our friend Don Ruh as Zena Halpern had done a year earlier. Scott was somewhat amused by the threat as he had no intention of treating Don unfairly. Scott believed Spartan also knew this but issued the warning regardless. (Wolter, 2017)

Page 2.

enclosed. I would not consider using this item in any work that you and Don collaborate on.

I am also including a separate letter that details my knowing Mr. Jackson and having employed him in the company that I headed. You should note that besides installing surveillance equipment and perimeter alarms, burglar alarms and CCTV, analog, we also had a printing company that provided printing to various private and commercial businesses located in Hartsdale N. Y. A Machine Shop Located in the Bronx N. Y. as well as a number of other enterprises off shore in England, Italy, France, Germany, Japan and Holland.

While Don and I no longer are in touch with each other I am still apprised of his activities by associates in the U. S. I understand that he has finally taken someone's advice seriously and wrote a book himself. I feel he has some skill in this field and am looking forward to reading it. It has been also brought to my attention that you have encouraged him in that regard. Hopefully that will provide you both with some financial remuneration. We shall be carefully watching to see if he receives a fair amount for all of the material he is providing you with for a repeat of Ms. Z. H's antics will not be tolerated. Further at the end of Mr. David Brody's Cult of Venus book he mentions that you are proposing a television series "Hoax or History". If it is your intention to gather the late Bill Jackson's material and then attempt to debunk it on national television to Don's discredit I would not take kindly to such a situation.

Sincerely,

D. P. Spartan

P. S. A copy of this letter and additional enclosed material shall be forwarded to Mr. Ruh also. I have informed my Depot Agents to disguise the senders and repackage the material as they see fit.

CHAPTER 5:

THE NECK MAP AND THE SINCLAIR JOURNALS

This next chapter presents the first of two new maps of Oak Island from the Cremona Document material which the world has never seen before. This chapter also presents relevant parts of incredible journal entries by multiple members of two prominent Scottish clans over a period of 417 years. Let's start with Sinclair/Wemyss journals.

In July of 2016, I was contacted by a distant relative of a man named John Weems who was born in 1741 and died in 1812. The woman claimed while doing genealogical research, she had found a total of twenty journals and a lambskin map inside a leather saddlebag, itself inside a wooden trunk stored at a home in Greenville, Tennessee. The first thirteen books were written in Latin, the next two in Old English and the last five in modern English. They spanned a time period of 417 years starting in 1353 with the last being written in 1770. The books were personal journals written about a secret mission carried out over a period of fifteen generations, five by the Sinclair Clan, and ten by the Wemyss/Weems Clan. The mission was called the "Covenant", which was sacred and highly secret mission carried out by the ideological and bloodline descendants of the fugitive Templar knights who escaped to Scotland from France prior to their suppression by the King of France and the Roman Catholic Church on October 13, 1307.

The journals tell the incredible tale of how the fugitive Templars assisted King Robert the Bruce of Scotland when his army defeated the British at the battle of Bannockburn in 1314. Because of their valiant service in this historic battle, the Scottish Earls were obligated to provide refuge and protection to the fugitive knights and their families who hid in the Wemyss Caves along the northern shore of the Firth of Forth for at least eight decades until in 1395 and 1398, Earl Henry Sinclair brought the treasures the Templars escaped to Scotland with, and the descendants of those knights to the "Western Lands". The mission is best summarized in this entry by Earl Henry Sinclair (1345-1404) on May 25, 1395:

> We leave this daybreak from Kirkwall for the western banks with the blessing of King Robert [III] and with the support of the hirdmen who will oversee my obligations in Orknades while I am gone. My brother David Sinclair, son of Isabella, and my eldest son Henry will govern in Rosslin with the assistance of my very capable wife and his brother John who oversees Hjatland.
>
> Our goal is to find a better route to the empires of China further south than the ice-covered lakes and suitable land for settlement beyond the boundaries of Groenland [Greenland] which we visit on our journey. We also travel with 120 remaining Knights Templars, descendants of those at Bannockburn under my grandfather's rule in search of a free Templar state. We search for suitable places to transfer the Templar treasure hidden in Scotland.
>
> The weather is exceptional this day and we have assembled a fleet of 8 ships: 4 galleys and 4 barques. As we visit Groenland and Reykjavik we will gather additional fishing vessels. Among our retinue is Nicolo and Antonio Zeno from Venice who are experts in navigating these seas. We intend to stop at Reykjavik to speak with the Althing[20] to gain their support for our journey in the name of Queen Margaret, as well as stores for our journey. Then we will visit the settlement in Groenland and the monastery there.
>
> I will miss my family while gone but trust in God and the King to protect them in my absence.

This stunning entry is remarkable for a number of reasons, but for the purposes of the Oak Island story it provides corroborating evidence of the extensive activities that took place underground as told in the encrypted messages in the Cremona Document material to be presented in the next chapter. It also confirms the date when these activities took place—creating

---

20 https://en.wikipedia.org/wiki/Althing

a hideaway for the vast wealth and vitally important artifacts the Templars wanted to keep safe for someday. That date was the year 1390.

Subsequent entries by Earl Henry share details about their activities during the nearly four months they spent in Nova Scotia and sites extending as far south as Cape Cod and Narraganset Bay in what is now Rhode Island. Those details include the following:

1. Their attempt to relocate members of a Templar party that traveled to the Western Lands in 1358: "*We will continue on to Western Lands with 8 ships to relocate the remaining Templars who came in 1358.*"

2. The return of a gravely ill Italian navigator, Nicolo Zeno, who died before arriving back to Scotland: "*Bad weather continues, and Nicolo has taken ill due to the coldness of the weather. Captain Nicolo returns to Orkney, but Captain Antonio and his men will journey with us to the Western Lands.*"

3. To map the coastline of Nova Scotia and the northeastern seaboard: "*We will rest for 2 days and then head south along the coast to find evidence of our Brethren and to map the coastline.*"

4. Losing two of their ships and scores of men in a violent storm: "*We have found the remains of the Repostus in the middle of a large bay just to the south of where the storm has deposited us. There are no signs of survivors, and the mast of the ship is floating broken on the sea. Several bodies have washed up on a nearby island and we can only suppose that the remainder of our Brethren have drowned.*"

5. Rescuing Antonio Zeno and the survivors of wrecked ship, Persephone: "*We have arrived at a sand island in the shape of the waning moon where 23 men await their rescue. Captain Zeno survives and tells us of how the ship was grounded on the reef and after a week was broken apart by the waves. Six men have drowned but the rest of his men have salvaged the supplies from the ship and have awaited rescue. We are happy that we are able to find them.*"

6. A summary of the mission upon his return to Scotland: "*We have returned from the Western Lands with 5 ships, having left 65 Templari and 2 ships in the New World. One will explore the northern passage to the inner seas and the other has been given the mission of exploring the eastern coast of the Western Lands and establishing a small colony.*"

7. Notably absent are details about their activities on Oak Island present-ed in the newly acquired Cremona Document material. Only a cryptic mention of surveying a selection of islands where they would later hide treasures, including on Oak Island, brought over three years later in 1398: *"We have concluded our survey of the bay and have identified at least 10 islands that are suitable for our plans. Captain Zeno has finished mapping the islands that we have chosen and has assured me that he will be able to find them again when we return."*

These amazing entries confirm and corroborate the information in the new Cremona Document material leaving out important details Earl Henry did not want the Church and Crowns in England and France to know about. The details of those activities in the new material were written by a different a hand by someone who had first-hand knowledge of what happened on Oak Island because he was there.

The Sinclair/Wemyss journals flesh out the previously unknown history of the secret and sacred mission of the Covenant that was handed off from the Weems Clan and Freemasonry to the Founding Fathers. On May 14, of 1769 when a twenty-eight-year-old John Weems received a message from his father who lived in what is now Abington, Pennsylvania, which was a province before America was founded. John Sr. wrote his son it was very important to meet with him as soon as possible (repeated from pages 8-9 for the reader's convenience):

"A courier arrived today from Philadelphia and my father has requested that I return home to deal with an important family matter. My father has never asked anything of me before, so I feel obligated to attend. He has insisted that I stop in Staunton and solicit Brother John Scott to accompany me as Mother has been ill and she wishes to see him. My brother-in-law Richard Gott and sister Margaret have agreed to look after Kitty and my small family in my absence. I hope to be gone only a few weeks and will leave in the morrow to do his bidding."

Ten days later May 24, 1769, John Jr. put his thoughts to paper about the important mission he was given about the Covenant he was now a part of that begin over four centuries earlier:

"It has taken hours to put my hand to pen and write my thoughts. I now understand why Father has taught us to write our thoughts each evening. Not only do we chronicle the events in our lives, but he has been preparing us for the adventure ahead. When I asked why he did not invite my brother Thomas he replied that although he loved his sons equally Thomas is a slave owner and might be swayed by the prospects of riches. Whereas I, am satisfied with my life and do not seek to put myself above other men. I am not certain that I agree with his assessment but will try to do my best to fulfill his wishes.

Father has always taught us that we are the descendants of great kings and queens in Scotland. Father is the grandson of the Earl of Wemyss, the Grandmaster of the Freemasons in Edinburgh. As such he bears the responsibility of a great family. When Thomas and I were of age we were initiated into the Freemasons in Philadelphia and so began our training in trades that would benefit both our country and our lives. I have been trained as a surveyor and engineer while Thomas claims his occupation as a blacksmith and metal worker. We are both educated men although our interests differ.

Father's story of our families' involvement in Freemason activities is confusing and lengthy. He has promised that as I read the journals of my ancestors who have gone before me that I will begin to under-stand the enormity of my journey. He has put into my safekeeping a small chest of journals that reach back hundreds of years requesting that I begin with the oldest. It is only then that I will understand what the Freemasons and the Templars before them have kept hidden and the efforts taken to preserve it. The Brethren have always kept such secrets and I have heard rumors for years but have given them no heed until now.

Father is concerned with the current political happenings and has received word that settlers have begun to settle the area of Nova Scotia where we must travel. He has arranged for us to leave on board ship in the morrow for Cape Breton where we are to seek out an alliance with others who would support our cause. My Uncle John Scott will accompany me as he did my father many years ago and acquaint me with the hiding place of what Father refers to only as the Covenant.

*He has also demanded that I record my journey so that someday I
may pass the responsibility along to my own son.*
The journey begins."

John then traveled to Nova Scotia to check on the treasures hidden by
Earl Henry Sinclair and his men nearly four centuries before, just as nine
generations of his ancestors, and three generations of Sinclair's, did before
him. Although there is no specific mention of Oak Island in either Earl
Henry's journals or John Weems' journals, we find it extremely compelling
the exact dates mentioned on the Neck Map are connected to when treasure
was hidden, and then recovered, match the journals' entries exactly, 1395
and 1769. Now let's take a closer look at the Neck Map.

DAN SPARTAN AFFIDAVIT

Before delving into specifics about the map, we need to add a little
context about where it came from and why it is now copied onto wrapping
paper. On March 4, 2021, Don received a black wooden box with gold trim
from the wife of his dear friend and colleague he'd known since High School
who had just passed away from sepsis, Daniel Spartan. Dan was scheduled
to have a chronically problematic knee amputated after two failed replace-
ments on February 21, 2021. Fearing he might not survive the surgery; Dan
prepared the box for Don just in case. Sadly, the brilliant man I never had
the pleasure of meeting, who a few years had cheekily threatened my life,
died the day before his scheduled surgery.

Don called me with the news about Dan and the box. As mentioned
earlier, within a few days, Janet and I drove to New York to open the puzzle
box with a local film crew recording the event. Dan had included several
interesting items and true to form, he saved the best for last. At the bottom
of the box was a large, folded piece of paper roughly 3 feet by 2 feet in size
that was taped together in the middle that put the first thing we pulled from
the box into context. Not only had Dan prepared the box just in case, but he
also had the foresight to include an affidavit explaining the two maps in the
box had been copied from a large rotting animal skin map onto wrapping
paper before it was lost. Once again Dan Spartan was one step ahead of
everyone, knowing how important the information was to both of us.

Page 01 (Hide)

To Whom it may Concern

On August 24th 1994 I received from Mr. William D. Jackson a large animal hide measuring approximately two feet by three feet with an additional section of the nape of the neck being eighteen inches by eleven inches. This hide had been fleshed and had the hair removed. It appeared to be of reindeer, caribou or elk. It had been tanned possibly with hickory wood but that is not certain. One side had lines presumably depicting land masses, coastlines, rivers and other prominent land features including in one instance an outline of a man made structure all burned into the hide with some type of heated tool. The places where the tool was first applied to the hide left darker thicker marks than elsewhere. It is possible that several tools were used in the undertaking as the widths of the lines varied. The nape portion requiring minute lines of what has been identified as the Eastern side of a portion of Nova Scotia must have had a fine tool. The hide itself is from .0781 to .0938 inches thick and when received was folded twice. Once making a size of one and one half feet by two feet with the nape tucked in and then again making one and one half feet by one foot. The entire hide was then rolled up to a tight bundle of slightly over one foot in diameter. The hide was then held in a bronze container one foot plus one quarter of one inch round with walls of one eighth inch to three sixteenths thick and thirteen inches long. There was a three inch long section that slid over the open top that had at its open end two one quarter inch slots one half inch up and one hundred eighty degrees apart. These slots engaged two bronze pins similarly placed on the lower section so that the slots when turned locked the upper portion in place. There was a bail at the closed end to allow the container to be carried. There was text on both sides of the hide. On the side with the burnt lines, the fleshed side, the writing was in several languages three of which were identified as Latin, Hebrew and French with the French being dominant. The writing appeared to have been done with a stylus or quill and made with what was thought to be oak gall ink but this proved to be only true of the text on the rear portion. All else was made with Walnut hulls and water boiled to a thin paste and alum added. In many places the ink had disappeared but the impression of the stylus into the hide remained as seen either with 3200 ang. Ultraviolet light or an electron microscope with 800 magnification.

The hide was kept in my place of residence in ███████████ for three years and then transferred to an external unheated shed adjacent to the houseboat on which we moved belonging to my wife's grandfather having been left to her on his passing. In 2010 we noticed that an odor was being emitted by the hide and it was found to be molded. This was probably due to the hot humid often wet climate of the region. We cleaned the mold with warm water and then dried the hide. It was then decided to copy the drawn and textual material of the hide onto paper and dispose of the hide. Since the hide was too large to fit on the light box attached to the drafting table in our machine shop we removed the nape and the hide proper was cut at the one and one half foot fold making two pieces of one and one half foot by two feet. When the light was turned on it revealed that the hide was translucent. My son whose eyesight was better than mine

This page and next: Dan Spartan prepared a detailed affidavit explaining how it took six months for he and his son to copy a rotting 3' by 2' sized animal skin map onto wrapping paper using a light table in 2010. The neck portion of the map was copied onto a separate piece of paper and was found wrapped in tin foil inside a secret compartment at the bottom of the puzzle box. (Courtesy of Donald Ruh)

The large map we labeled "Map 8", contained thirteen individual maps of locations where treasure had been hidden over the centuries by the Knights Templar order. A second smaller map was found wrapped in tin foil inside a secret compartment in the bottom of the box. This map was a

Page 02. (Hide)

accepted the job of copping the material onto the paper we had from wrapped items received at the shop. The work began in October of 2009 and was completed in March of 2010. The two halves of the work were then joined with clear tape so that the document was restored to its original size. My son was meticulous in his transferring the text on both sides of the work. We often conversed as to what certain letters and characters were as the writing was odd and often obscure. The lettering was odd. It was often difficult to ascertain the letters A from I and the N was written backwards. The U was curled on the left only and the C and the S had curlicues on the upper portions. There were both upper and lower case letters in the same word. This was thought to be some kind of cryptic design possibly a code but alas our Cryptographer, Mr. David Rian, had passed away. The original was burnt.

It was an interesting and often exasperating task. The finished product was rolled into a tube one and one half inches in diameter closed at both ends with wooden plugs and stored in our safe in the shop. The nape section was rolled up and covered with aluminum foil and kept separately. I have named four persons to inherit this document upon my passing, Mr. Donald A Ruh of Dover Plains, NY. USA, Ms. Zena Halpern of Woodbury NY. USA, Mr. Maximillian Finkenburg of Auckland, Australia and Mr. Scott Wolter of Chanhassen, MN, USA in that order of importance and surviving me.

My signature below attests to the above as being accurate and true. The initials of my son are also included below mine. My wife and our engineer in the shop in ███ one hundred and fifty miles up the ███ river from our houseboat home.

D. Spartan

Daniel Spartan

D.S.

Daniel Spartan Jr.

Leela Kaukthi Spartan
Witness 1 Mrs. Spartan

Soomong Tan Nag
Witness 2 Soomong Tan Nag

January 4, 2021

detailed drawing of the southern part of Nova Scotia with several comments written in French and three dates written in Roman numerals. Even as over-whelmed as we all were by the incredible artifacts and documents Spartan had placed in the box, we were still able to recognize Mahone Bay on the map and a line drawn from two closely spaced islands in the unmistakable location of Oak Island. This caught us by surprise as it is depicted as a single island today with the now famous "swamp" in the middle. However, geologists say the island was actually two islands in the past suggesting the map

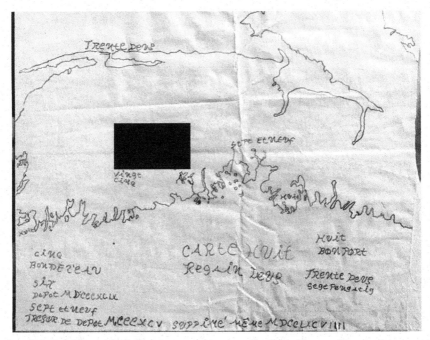

Inside the puzzle box left for Don by Dan Spartan, was a paper map copied from an older animal skin map was a detailed sketch of Nova Scotia. In the Mahone Bay area of the map we named the "Neck Map", were two closely spaced islands drawn that can only be what is now known as Oak Island. A line drawn from the islands with French words matched the same words at the bottom of the map. In short, the words said treasure was deposited in 1395, "deleted"/recovered in 1769. (Courtesy of Donald Ruh)

was originally drawn hundreds of years ago. The line drawn from the islands extends upward to the beginning of three French words, *Sept Et Neuf* (Seven And Nine). These same words appear at the bottom of the map along with the words and dates, *"Tresor de depot"* (Deposit of Treasure) MCCCXCV (1395); *"Suppime' Même"* (Delete Even) MDCCLX[C]VIII (1769). "Delete Even" can only mean the treasure that was once there was "deleted" or recovered, which we now know to be correct. This map was the first time we had a definite answer the burning question people have pondered for over two centuries. These dates correspond with the Sinclair/Wemyss journals of when Earl Henry and his men were there and when John Weems also went to check on the treasures in 1769 which is when we know the treasures were recovered. Now that we know when the treasure on Oak Island and other locations were recovered, let's turn to one fascinating example of what the treasure was used for.

This portrait of Gilbert du Montier, Marquis de La Fayette (1757-1834) depicts the famous French, Revolutionary War general as he would have looked during his visit to Fayetteville, North Carolina, on March 4th and 5th, 1825. Oil on Canvas by William C. Fields, III. (Wolter, 2021)

CHAPTER 6:

LAFAYETTE'S LOOT

The 400-year-long mission of the Templar's and their ideological descendants to create a Free Templar State they called the "Covenant" was an incredible plan that was eventually realized resulting in what is now called the United States of America. Between the Cremona Document and the Sinclair/Wemyss journals we know much about when and where the Templar treasures were hidden in North America. What we know very little about is what the treasures were used for. In July of 2020, Don received a small, wooden puzzle box from the estate of John Lennon, an agent who was associated with persons in Scotland Yard and assisted Don and his colleagues whenever they traveled to the United Kingdom. The box was left to Lennon by Bill Jackson in 1996. Inside the box was a treasure hunt for Don that we decided to pursue that resulted in an exciting, unexpected discovery.

This parcel of treasure was apparently left by the colonists as payment to the famous French general Gilbert du Montier, Marquis de La Fayette (1757-1834) who served in the Revolutionary War in America (1777 to 1781) and the French Revolutions (1791 through 1797).[21] He was heralded as a hero when he visited and toured the new Republic addressing the U.S. House of Representatives in December of 1824. The cryptic message Bill Jackson left for Don suggested a treasure had been hidden for La Fayette in the late 18th Century. The big question weighing on our minds, and on Bill Jackson's mind back in 1996 was, is that treasure still there? After a brief discussion amongst ourselves we agreed there was only one way to find out.

---

21 https://www.britannica.com/biography/Marquis-de-Lafayette/The-French-Revolution

MAP 8, SECTION 13

Among the massive trove of research materials Don received from Bill Jackson was an undeveloped roll of film. Don had the film developed in 2013 and it contained 25 pictures including several images of four detailed maps: Nova Scotia, Southern Connecticut, Narragansett Bay, and Cape Cod. One question that has nagged us about the Cremona Document since the now-iconic Nova Scotia map appeared in the photos from the film roll is, how many maps were there? It wasn't until December of 2019 when Don received the two pages of notes from Dr. Bill Jackson, via the bequest of John Drake, that we realized there were at least _eight_ maps. The notes pages were a revelation for many reasons. However, it was with the second package Don received from his colleague, John Lennon, that the murky Cremona Document story started getting clearer.

XL VISITEZ LA CARTE HVIT POUR LE LOCAL DE NOUS EFFORTS POUR CACHER LES TRÉSORS DE L'ORDRE. NOUS COMMENÇONS LA CONSTRUCTION.

On page two of the note's pages Don Ruh shared with Scott in December of 2019, there was an out of sequence note labeled number forty. "(XL) 40. Visit map eight for the locale of our efforts to hide the treasures of order. We are starting construction." (Courtesy of Donald Ruh)

This chapter of the story began with a cryptic two-sentence email I received from Don on May 13, 2020: _"I got an odd letter yesterday. Mailed you a copy today with copy of the envelope."_ On May 18, 2020, I opened Don's letter and inside were copies of the envelope, the letter, and a picture of a group of men that included only the third picture of Dr. Bill Jackson I had ever seen. The letter was written by Mr. J. McMasters and contained the arrangements for a box to be delivered to Don in June, as well as personal information about Mr. Dan Spartan that is not relevant to our story. What is relevant is transcribed here:

> _Dear Sir,_
>
> _Mrs. Elizabeth Anne Lennon contacted Mrs. Lialla ▮▮▮▮_
> _yesterday with a request to have a package delivered to you via a dead_
> _drop or depot agent. Her husband who recently received damage to_
> _his larynx put the following arrangements in place._
>
> _Mrs. Anita ▮▮▮ visiting relatives in Sweden and caught up in_
> _the COVID-19 situation in London, England, will be handed by Mrs._

Lennon a cardboard box about 12 inches long by 4 inches wide and high. She will board an airplane bound for Dallas, Texas, USA. Upon her arrival and after any quarantine requirements are met she will send the package via courier to Ms. Deborah ███████, *Depot for Ms. Julia* ████████. *Ms.* ███ *will travel by automobile with her husband to visit with two friends Ms. Nancy* ███ *and Ms. Caitlin* ███. *In Rhinebeck, New York, on the 24th of June for Ms.* ███ *birthday celebration to which you are invited and shall retrieve said package less its outer wrapper then. Additional invited guests shall be Mr. and Mrs.* ████, *Mr.* ███, *Ms. Dana* ██, *and Ms. Cassidy* ███.

Should these arrangements not be satisfactory to you please contact Ms. ████ *within 24 hours of June 24, 2020, and subsequent arrangements shall be devised.*

Very truly yours,

Mr. J. McMasters

After reading the letter I called Don to get his take. My first question was what did he think would be inside the package? In his deep raspy voice, Don said, "I have no idea, but it must be significant due to all the trouble they're planning to go through to get the box to me."

I agreed Dr. Jackson must've left something good for his best friend. I told Don whenever the box arrived, he had to promise not to open it until I could get there to film the moment. Don agreed, and then on June 19, 2020, Don sent an email explaining how the cardboard package we had anxiously awaited was delivered:

Hi Scott

Package arrived via Ms. Debbie and Mr. & Mrs. Ross. 9:47 AM 6/19/2020.

Mr. Ross stayed in the car. Mrs. Ross was her usual obnoxious self and I hardly recognized her from 9 years ago. Debbie put on a little weight but still looked great. We had a nice reunion. Debbie's husband is working in California and could not get away. She traveled with the Ross's, something akin to going to Hell and Back.

Box has had the outer wrapping with postage etc. removed. It is sealed with clear tape. OD [outside dimensions] measured 111/2 inches long by 91/8nches wide & 71/4nches high. It is 145/8nches on the diagonal. Photos below. Black dry marker writing on box says, "For Mr. Ruh." I cut a small portion of the tape at one corner and inserted a Lizard Cam probe. This has a black and white screen only. Revelation is some Styrofoam packaging, off-white paper packing and something resting diagonally wrapped in white/off-white paper.

Metal detector indicates presence of metal in upper left corner as seen in photo 2 of box. There is no magnetic action indicated by a magnet placed inside and around the box. I'll await your decision to film the further process of opening it. I can have this photographed if necessary.

Don

It was another month before I could get to Don's house, deciding to drive to New York from Minnesota during the height of the Covid-19 pandemic ravaging the nation at the time. It was a hot and muggy day on July 25, 2020, when I set up two video cameras and recorded Don opening the cardboard box. Anticipation was heightened as he pulled out a wooden puzzle box with dimensions of ten inches by three inches by one-and-a-half inches thick. Attached to the top of the box with a rubber band was a typed note signed by Dr. Bill Jackson. The note made clear Dr. Jackson's line of succession as to whom should receive the package had Don already passed away.

After reading the note, Don immediately went to work figuring out how to open the small puzzle box and within thirty seconds it was open. This was the fourth puzzle box I had seen Don work on and I knew by now he was an expert at opening them. The first thing he pulled out was typed letter written by Dr. Jackson dated October 12, 1994. As Don read the letter aloud, many missing pieces to the Cremona Document puzzle started to fall into place. Most notably, confirmation that there were indeed eight maps, and who Dr. Jackson had disseminated them to. We would soon learn more about the eighth map the letter made clear was comprised of multiple parts. In fact, we agreed the invisible map on the back of page one of the notes he'd shown me the previous December, was part of Map 8 since it pin-pointed the location of a treasure. In this case, it appears the treasure was most likely a land claim.

After reading Dr. Jackson's letter, Don turned his attention to a small metal cylinder wrapped in electrical tape. What emerged first after Don unscrewed its top was the small cylindrical key mentioned in the letter,

To Whom it man concern:

The enclosed wooden box is the property of Doctor William David Jackson being held in Trust by and under the Will of Mr. John D. Lennon for Mr. Donald Albert Ruh, Mr. Daniel Argos Spartan, Ms. Andria Arkinson Fox (leudaea), her cousin Martin Harold McCauley or Samantha Lyn Ryan. The order of succession as I have written it.

Very truly yours

Bill Jackson

The typed note was attached to the outside of the wooden box with Dr. William Jackson's signature. (2020)

October 12, 1994

Dear Brother Lennon

I was so pleased to hear from you and the good news that you are the father of a baby girl, Anne. May she be the joy of your life. Best wishes also to the proud mother, Elizabeth.

Your last letter mentioned that due to this happy event you would be making a new Will. I hope ypu will indulge me and add a clause that the enclosed wooden box should be held by you in trust for Mr. Donald A. Ruh to be delivered after your dimise.

The box contains a portion of the De Leon File that I sold through Mr Rhinhardt this past August. The recipient got four maps with the document of the eight included. Two went to other persons and one has been held in escrow by Mr. Spartan. Map eight I have copied off parts of it and have included in this box. The reason for that is the map is broken down into several parts each of which detail a different location where something of wealth was secreated. Some have been retrieved in the past and those parts of the map I have not copied out. What may remain is listed in the enclosed material for Mr. Ruh.

Don Ruh is the only person that took my research seriously and has helped me with it over the years so I include this portion to him but wish to do so after I have departed this earth. Since he is the youngest of the ████████ personnel I think he will survive long enough for the current political situation in America to have passed on leaving what I hope will be a more open government with less red tape.

I also want to thank you for suggesting Mr Lenord Ramsey as the person to decipher the obscure measurments for the key drawing that would fit the ceder lined box. Mr. Ramsey has done a wonderful job and I have sent his plan to Mr. Spartan's machine shop company resulting in the key enclosed in the waterproof container in the box you now hold in your hands. Hopefully Mr. Ruh will be able to fit into the lock should it ever be recovered from its burial place in America.

I also wish to thank you for your help with the ariel photographs of the location in America and the enlargements of the concerned sections. Also your gracious assistance with the securing of the material from the CCCCP group in Phliladelphia. These persons were not actually carpenters but were designers and archetects that built the buried box. I am still not sure how they were involved in this project.

Please confirm that you can do as I have requested above. If not also let me know that I may make other arrangements perhaps with Mr. Finkenberg in Australia.

As always best wishes for the future and don't sell the property in Ipswich. I think it is the most picturesque and beautiful place and is where you should consider retiring so that you can enjoy your hobby of painting when you finally retire.

Sincerely,

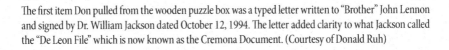

The first item Don pulled from the wooden puzzle box was a typed letter written to "Brother" John Lennon and signed by Dr. William Jackson dated October 12, 1994. The letter added clarity to what Jackson called the "De Leon File" which is now known as the Cremona Document. (Courtesy of Donald Ruh)

which was wrapped in two pieces of very thin paper as well as three other small sheets of paper. One of the pieces of paper contained hand-written drawings of the key with the very precise measurements that had been used to make it. Two other pieces of paper were aerial photographs with black ink Xs drawn in what appeared to open areas within wooded land. Where these wooded areas were was unknown, until Don opened the folded thin sheets of paper.

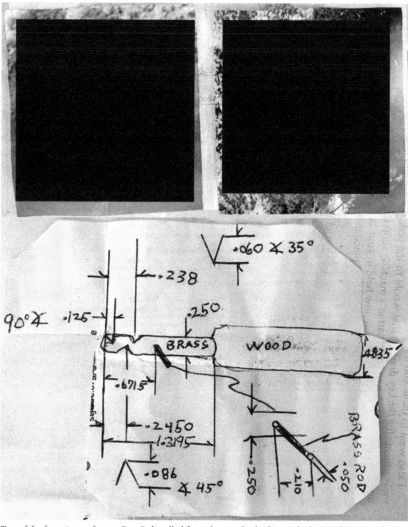

Two of the four pieces of paper Don Ruh pulled from the metal cylinder inside the wooden puzzle box he pulled from the cardboard box he had just opened. One contained the precise measurements necessary to make a key to apparently fit inside a wooden chest. (Wolter/Wolter, 2020)

As Don unrolled the first of two thin sheets of paper rolled up around the key, I recognized Theban letters that were the chosen alphabet used to create most of the Cremona Document. Once opened, numerous lines of Theban text were revealed along with several Roman numerals that turned out to be dates, and a location identified by latitude and longitude. After we finished recording Don opening the package, I had a chance to examine the Theban page carefully and noticed more symbols that would reveal additional information about a part of the story that meant nothing to either Don or me previously. At the top and bottom of the page were three inverted V-shaped symbols reminiscent of a working compass along with an carpenter's square symbol in the middle. There were also two five-pointed stars at the top of the page. At the bottom was what looked like a stylized fish symbol.

I then noticed a carefully placed symbol within one of the Roman numerals as if a watermark of authenticity, or a blessing. Within the date of 1724 (MDCCXXIV) on line three, in the second Roman numeral ten was a Hooked X—the only one on the entire page.

The second piece of paper was a map copied from another document in pencil by Dr. Jackson. Carefully drawn was what looked like a river with several small islands, one of which was circled with a line drawn to words on the side written in French, *Le Isle d'or* (The Isle of Gold). To the right of the river was what looked like an angel fish, but we correctly surmised it was a larger, detailed drawing of the *"The Golden Island."* At the bottom of the page, Dr. Jackson copied two more lines of French, *"Le carte huit regain trois"* (The eighth map, part three). As if the map wasn't exciting enough, it held one more surprise we didn't catch at first glance. The lower line of text was underlined with a stylized curve at the end with two additional short lines. Upon rotating the page ninety degrees counterclockwise, the familiar symbol jumped off the page—it was a cleverly placed Hooked X!

The Hooked X symbol is a sacred and secret symbol used by the Knights Templar cartographers that represented the essence of their ancient, true ideological beliefs in Monotheistic Dualism. It is the belief in a single Deity that has dualistic aspects of opposites that keep things in balance such as good-bad, light-dark, yin-yang, male-female, heaven and earth.

Don and I spent the next four hours working on the Theban page converting the symbols to letters, then into words. It was obvious the language was

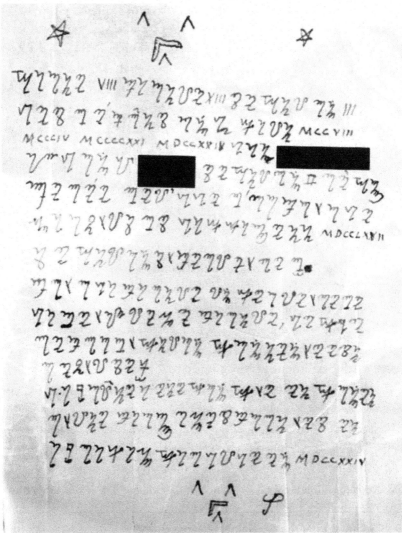

The first page Don unwrapped from around the key inside the wooden puzzle box contained fourteen lines of Theban script with several Roman numerals throughout. Two groups of three compasses with an carpenter's square symbol were at the top and bottom of the page along with two five-pointed star symbols at the top and a stylized fish symbol on the bottom right. On line three is another symbol carefully embedded within the Roman numeral date of 1724 as an apparent watermark of authenticity to those in the know, is the Hooked X. The coordinates of the location have been blacked out to protect the site from trespassers. (Courtesy of Donald Ruh)

French as we had been through this exercise with other documents before, most recently with the two pages of notes he received from John Drake's estate in December. It was a challenge as spaces between the words were not clear, so it took a while to finally translate the message from French into English. The problem then became choosing the right words as the translation program gave us multiple options. Eventually, we settled on the following translation:

> *Map 8, Part 13, Section 3. The deposits were made 1208, 1304, 1421, 1724. Latitude – degrees W,—minutes, Longitude – degrees, ▉ minutes N, Section 2. Recovered Island of gold for Marquis de Lafayette 1772. Upper section of map 8, for the lower part of the second part the key reproduction contained is necessary/required. The box was designed and constructed by James Portues and Abraham Carlile in 1724.*

Our minds were suddenly racing, trying to make sense of the message and it didn't take long for us to draw some reasonable conclusions. First, it was apparent there was a treasure—and possibly two, based on the aerial photos—buried out there that somehow involved the French General, Marquis de Lafayette, who helped lead our troops into battle against the British in the Revolutionary War. Could these treasures have been left for him as payment for his services to the Patriot cause? Second, what was the meaning of the four dates? My first thought was they were dates when Templar/Freemasonic treasures were brought over from Europe to be used for the eventual colonist's cause that was the Revolutionary War. This immediately recalled the four-centuries-long mission of the Templar's/Freemasonic effort of bringing Templar treasure to North America to be used to establish the sanctuary so masterfully detailed in the Sinclair/Wemyss journals. Could the treasure referenced in these pages be part of the Templar treasures brought to over centuries earlier? Making a payment to Lafayette for all he did for the early Republic would have been a good use of those funds.

The second part of the message refers to the cedar-lined box Dr. Jackson referred to in his letter, but it took some research to understand who James Portues and Abraham Carlile were, and what their

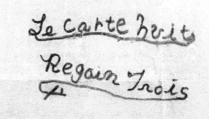

The second page contains a map copied by Dr. William Jackson of a river with small islands. One of the islands was circled and to the right was a detailed drawing of the island that would be our target for a treasure hunt. The two lines of French text at the bottom of the page were underlined; when rotated ninety degrees counterclockwise, the bottom line contained a cleverly placed Hooked X symbol! (Courtesy of Donald Ruh)

roles were in this story. The big break came when Don recalled the name Carlile in an eighteenth-century letter that until now, he thought had no relevance to the Cremona Document. That letter dated March 10, 1778, which addressed knowledge about the "brass device", presumably the same device found inside the decorative ornament Don discovered off Bannerman Island in 1968 that started this whole adventure. The letter was addressed to a Mister M. Vauxhall, Esq., and was signed, *"Your servant, CCCCP member, A. Carlile."* It was mention of the CCCCP that was key to solving this part of the mystery.

Don had already figured out the letters CCCCP stood for the Consolidated Carpenters of the City and County of Philadelphia. At that point, I jumped on my phone and quickly found the organization was a craft guild that was founded in 1724, one of the Roman numeral dates on the Theban page! From there we reasoned Portues and Carlile must have made the cedar-lined box Don now had the key to open. A little more online research and a phone call to the Carpenter's Hall resulted in a meeting the next day with the director, Michael Norris.

10 March 1778

M. Vauxhall, Esq.

I have this day received a letter from the Italian, M. Benvenuto, explaining the third and forth pages of the year we remember paper. He describes a system of ancient navigation by means of an odd device. This device having a wire basket upon it receives the metal plate engraved with the simbols for A, B, E, T, and O besides various constellations. The plate is retained in the wire frame with four small brass nail like pieces of triangular shape much as a common nail. These are placed into similar cuts in both the plate and the base below the wire basket. The top of the device is aligned with simbols to the stbd. and port of each letter by which the navigator has in his head certain stars of each that will reveal through the center hole a star that will guide the course across the waters from the dark continent to our home shores. The base of this device rests in some recess upon the deck of the vessel all so secured to prevent movement from the sway of the vessel upon the sea. The triangle shaped cuts are so arranged as to be one compass point apart thus making 32 cuts about the circle and a point due north. No variation for the angle of the sun is so allowed thus making for significant error over the long voyage yet owing to the size of the land mass it could little be missed. Page three also shows the device with a smaller disk centered about a central pin with 40 lines radiating from the center culminating in small circles in which a pin is placed in accordance with the cycle of Venus.

Shall I replace this with the cryptic form to be included with the other pages you have sent me? I await your reply before continuing with my commission.

Your servant, CCCCP member

A. Carlile

This transcription of a letter written by Abraham Carlile that was part of Bill Jackson's research material and contains interesting information pertaining to the Cremona Document and the treasure hunt Bill left for Don. M. Benvenuto must be a descendant of one of the two authors of the pamphlet published in 1715 which Bill Jackson purchased in 1971 that contained the name "Onteora", a name etched on one of the inserts found inside the brass device, and referenced the document titled, "A Year We Remember." Bill then purchased the document from perhaps another descendant named Gustavo Benvenuto. This letter is interesting in that it implies important people who were involved in the Revolution in Philadelphia were also aware of the Cremona Document and the Templar treasures hidden centuries earlier. (Courtesy of Donald Ruh)

Mr. Norris was very accommodating and gave me a tour and talked about the history of the building where secret meetings were held by people like Ben Franklin during the leadup to the Revolution. What caught my eye immediately were the framed historical banners of the Carpenter Company with familiar symbols arranged exactly like those on the Theban page. Mr. Norris also showed me lists of the founding and early members and both James Portues and Abraham Carlile were listed.

After thanking Mr. Norris for his kindness and assistance, I jumped in my truck and drove off satisfied these new pieces to the Cremona Document story were fitting together. I also had confirmation it was indeed a living document comprised of parts from the early and late twelfth, late fourteenth, and now the late seventeenth centuries—during the Revolutionary War. The other realization is the document essentially chronicles the historical transition of the fugitive medieval Templars into modern Freemasonry that included the Founding Fathers who obviously knew all about the early Templar activity on the continent and the treasures they left behind. What also became apparent was this latest chapter in the Cremona Document story dovetails with the Sinclair/Wemyss Journals breathing veracity into both sets of documents.

On July 27, 2020, Scott visited the Carpenter's Company in Philadelphia and saw multiple historical banners with the same three compasses and square symbols in their Coat of Arms as drawn on the Theban page. (Wolter 2020)

Colonial Philadelphia took shape in the hands of Company members.

Here is a sampling from founding members.

James Portues — Arrived with William Penn on the ship "Welcome" and is one of ten who founded the Company in 1724. He built a slate roofed house on 2nd Street near Walnut, where Penn later lived. Site is now "Welcome Park"

Edmund Wooley — Built Independence Hall, a 20-year project, that in 1750 was America's largest building.

Joseph Harrison — A founding member of the Company who with John, his son, completed two early Swedish Lutheran (now Protestant Episcopal) churches: Holy Trinity in Wilmington, Delaware, and Gloria Dei in Philadelphia.

A Sampling from early members.

Samuel Rhoads — Built Pennsylvania Hospital, the nation's first. He was elected mayor of Philadelphia while a delegate to the First Continental Congress.

Samuel Griscom — A house carpenter whose claim to fame is his daughter, Elizabeth (later Betsy Ross.) She attended the Quaker school marked by the brick wall just west of the Hall. Her grandfather, Tobias, was also a member.

Joseph Fox — A builder who inherited wealth, Fox lent the Company 1,300 to complete the Hall. As president, he hosted meetings leading to the First Continental Congress. British troops burned his country home, destroying early Company records.

Benjamin Loxley — Lumber merchant and developer, Captain Loxley recruited four Company members as officers in his rapid strike force, known as a "flying camp."

Abraham Carlile — A prosperous lumber merchant who provided material for the Hall's construction. He was hanged in 1778 for traitorous activity during British occupation of the city.

Robert Smith — Built Carpenters' Hall, Christ Church steeple and 50 other projects. America's foremost architect-builder died of pneumonia while building fortifications for the city.

Gunning Bedford — Created two 40-foot triumphal arches at 5th and Market Streets. The first (1784) marked the end of the Revolution; the second (1788) celebrated ratification of the Constitution. His portrait is on the opposite wall.

Thomas Nevell — Built Mount Pleasant, a magnificent country mansion still standing in Fairmount Park. He began the nation's first architecture school in his south 4th Street home.

Matthew McGlathery — Major supplier of gun carriages for cannon used by the Continental Army. Portrait by his son-in-law, Raphaelle Peale, is at the left.

Thomas Procter — Built the City Tavern, largest hotel in North America. Lt. Col. of artillery in Continental Army; later Brig. General in militia.

William Williams — Built the "Grand Federal Edifice," a float drawn by six horses for the parade celebrating ratification of the Constitution, July 4, 1788. He was a Lt. Col. in the Continental Army.

In the Revolution, half the membership of 65 saw active duty in the militia or Continental Army. Others built gun carriages and the city's fortifications.

Both James Portues and Abraham Carlile who were named in the Theban page are also listed on this picture listing the names of founding and early members of the Carpenter's Company. (Wolter 2020)

CAMPBELL ISLAND, NORTH CAROLINA

The Theban page, dating to the late seventeenth century, also contained a latitude and longitude that required no adjustment—unlike the Nova Scotia map dating to 1179 requiring an adjustment of 2.5 degrees for Paris as the prime meridian as opposed to Greenwich, England. When plotted on Google Earth it landed on the Cape Fear River near Wilmington, North Carolina. My eyes widened as I instantly recognized that the river on the screen just south of Wilmington matched the map from the puzzle box perfectly. I then scrolled in on the island circled on the map and the "angel fish"-shaped island on the right side of the map page immediately jumped out.

I then turned my attention to the two aerial photographs from the puzzle box with X's apparently marking where the cedar-lined box was buried. To my amazement, I was able to find both locations on the island after only a few minutes of searching. The next step was to figure out if the island was public or private land, and if private land, who were the owners? Janet quickly went to work and within a couple of hours figured out the island was private land owned by a family trust named Trask which owned extensive property in the area. She also found a telephone number to the office of the Trask family's real estate development company, handed it to me and said, "Good luck with the call."

I was a little apprehensive thinking about what I was going to say, but the woman who answered the phone was very friendly and heard me out. Surprisingly, she was very receptive and said she'd have Mr. Webster Trask contact me, which he did the next day. Mr. Trask could not have been a kinder, more reasonable person who was happy to work with us to reach an agreement to allow a treasure hunt. Within a few weeks on October 1, 2020. We had a signed agreement and a plan to drive to North Carolina. Janet and I drove from Minnesota, Don drove from his home in Dover Plains, and cameraman Tom Colvin flew in from Denver to document the search. On November 13, we all arrived in Wilmington and checked into a hotel. That night we met with representatives of the Trask Family—Lee Singleton, Hal Kitchen, and his son Henry—to go over plans for the next day. Don shared the documents from the puzzle box and explained the story to everyone as Tom was rolling recording the moment.

Donald Ruh holds a wooden puzzle box as he tells the Cremona Document story to members of the Trask Family on November 13, 2020. (Wolter, 2020)

Everyone arrived at the public dock in Wilmington at 9:00 a.m. and loaded two boats with gear, then we all hopped in for the five-mile ride down the Cape Fear River to Campbell Island. Lee Singleton, driver of the boat carrying Don, Janet, myself, and Tom, carefully approached the first location on the northern end of the island covered with trees, vines and underbrush. We quickly unloaded the packs, shovels, wooden screen for sifting, the metal detector, and the drone, and placed them on the shore. From there, I was able to locate the clearing in the aerial photograph and then sent the drone into the air to confirm we were on the right spot. Satisfied we were on the correct "X" in the aerial photograph, I made a twelve-foot diameter circle around what I felt was the exact site, stuck a shovel in the sand and said, "This is the spot gang, let's start digging."

My plan of action was to dig out the circled area roughly one foot deep and then smooth out the bottom to look for evidence of a disturbance in the sand indicating a previous burial. Janet had already used the metal detector in the area and found only small metallic debris such as bottle caps and fishing lures that had been washed onto the island, likely during flooding from hurricanes. While we shoveled out the area Janet, armed with the metal detector, swept around the clearing. She found a few more bits of modern debris, and then she hit on something that seemed more interesting. Unable to find the item feeling in the sand, she called Don over, who had a hand-held metal detector, and asked for his assistance. Don also got a hit but was unable to locate the item in the sand. At that point, they decided to shovel the sand into the screen to see if that would help. Once the wet sand was loaded into the screen, Janet waved the metal detector over the hole to make sure the item was safely in the screen, and she heard nothing.

Meanwhile I was just finishing smoothing out the bottom of my one-foot deep, twelve-foot diameter hole when I heard some excitement coming from Don and Janet who were hovering over the sifting screen. Then I heard Janet yell something that made me sprint right over, "A coin, we found a coin!" A moment later she yelled, "1790!" Tom's camera was rolling as he also sprint-ed over to capture the moment. Everybody else ran over as Janet pulled the sand covered coin from the screen and handed it to me. Sure enough, it was a coin alright and the 1790 date was clear as could be.

A very excited Janet Wolter holds the Dutch East India Company coin dated 1790, over the spot where it was found while metal detecting. (2020)

A close-up of the coin seconds after Janet Wolter found it with assistance from Donald Ruh on Campbell Island on the Cape Fear River, near Wilmington, North Carolina. (2020)

The excitement of the coin discovery was palpable among our group and seemed to tell us we were on the right track. Once we caught our breath, I went back to the circle I had dug out and looked carefully again for evidence of a previous burial. Before concluding there wasn't anything there, I checked the circle from directly overhead with the drone and found nothing. After three hours of digging, metal detecting, and sifting through dozens of shovelsfull of sand, we decided it was time to move on to the second location on the south end of the island.

It was nearly 1:00 p.m. and low tide as Janet and I hiked the quarter-mile through the swampy part of the island, while the others shuttled over in the boats. Once we reached the trees at the second spot of higher ground, I immediately started looking for the spot on the second aerial photo with an "X". After about 15 minutes the GPS on my phone put me on the spot. As I walked to the location, I realized I was standing in a small depression reminiscent of a collapsed box—like the depression over an old grave where the coffin had decomposed and collapsed. I called out for Janet to sweep the area with the metal detector, and she immediately went to work. The detector went wild buzzing as she waved the unit over the depression. Every-one suddenly froze, and it took a few seconds for everyone holding a shovel to frantically start digging. The hole grew quickly in size and after a few minutes Lee Singleton thrust his shovel in and we all heard a dull thud. He had hit something hard.

There was a collective pause for a few seconds, then the digging continued in earnest. As the hole expanded, water began to flood the space, I kneeled and put my hands into the hole trying to feel the object beneath the water. A moment later I felt the straight edge of what felt like a box. This news raised the intensity of the digging and excitement we might have found a treasure box. After roughly fifteen minutes of frantic digging and my tugging at the metallic object I was finally able to pry it loose and pull it from the hole. To our dismay, it wasn't a treasure box. What we had discovered was a two-foot-long piece of metal with a heavy layer of iron oxide corrosion covering it. Given the history that the island was used as a practice bombing target during World War II, the metal was most likely a piece from a large bomb that was not live.

The group stood in stunned silence realizing we weren't going to find the cedar-lined treasure box we were hoping for. The sun was setting, and we all knew it was time to make our way back to Wilmington. It had been an exhilarating day and we all pondered the significance of the coin we found at the first site. It didn't take long to figure out the coin had been minted by the Dutch East India Company. It was also apparent the coin showed a fair amount of wear, meaning it had been in circulation after 1790 for at least a few years. Numerous scenarios ran through our heads about how the coin could have ended up where we found it. However, since there has never been development on the island and due to its remote location, it seems highly unlikely to be a random event from people having been there in recent times and losing or intentionally dropping a late eighteenth-century coin. Because the Dutch East India Company stopped minting coins when the company was dissolved in 1799, it stands to reason the duit coin went out of use shortly thereafter. Therefore, what seems most plausible is the coin was accidentally left by a group who visited the island at a time when the currency was most likely still in use; probably to recover or place the cedar-lined treasure chest sometime between 1790 and 1800.

A couple weeks after the trip I called Don on his seventy-eighth birthday to talk about the coin and get his thoughts on why Dr. Jackson had included two aerial photographs of different parts of the island when there was only one cedar-lined treasure box. Don paused and said, "I knew Bill very well

Scott Wolter hammers off the heavy iron oxide crust on the surface of a piece of steel pulled from the hole dug at the second site on Cambell Island. The piece of steel is believed to be part of a bomb dropped during World War II when the island was used as a bombing target. (Wolter, 2020)

and he had connections with the military through our company where he was able to get the photographs. He probably also had access to technology that was able to document good-sized metal deposits and the two photos marked with the "X" were likely the biggest hits on the island."

I hadn't thought about technology locating metal concentrations but knew the treasure box could only be at one spot. Don continued:

> Because the military had used the island to practice aerial bombing, and the Trask Family didn't purchase the island until 1980, the military would have to have swept the island to remove the remains of the bombing before the island could be sold. And because the metal detecting technology prior to 1980 could only penetrate the ground about twelve inches, the piece of metal we found around eighteen inches deep in the ground was probably the metallic hit Bill got back in the early 1990's. That means the treasure had to have been at the first location where we found the coin. To me, that means the coin is probably connected to the treasure. Exactly how and when the two are connected is anybody's guess.

I thought about his argument for a while and came to the same conclusion. Don's logic was sound, but there was another reason I believe the treasure was at the first location that had nothing to do with technology or the coin. When I went back and looked at the map Dr. Jackson had traced in pencil from part thirteen of Map 8, I noticed a very subtle but important clue. There was an oval-shaped area marking the northern site that corresponded with one of the aerial photographs marked with an "X". Inside the oval-shaped area was a dot, the only dot marked on the island, likely marking where the cedar-lined treasure box was originally buried.

BILL JACKSON AND THE CAMPBELL ISLAND TREASURE
(Commentary by Donald Ruh)

> On page 99 is the letter sent to me that was originally sent to Mr. John Lennon in October of 1994, from Bill Jackson. It states in paragraph four as follows, "Don Ruh is the only person that took my research seriously and helped me with it over the years, so I include this portion to him but wish to do so after I have departed this earth." The items mentioned were a map of an island in a river, two arial photographs with one place on each marked with an X, and a detailed sketch of what was described as a key with an actual reproduction of that drawing.

While I was obviously interested in the material and thought it was another piece to the complicated puzzle with regards to his research, I cannot say that I was optimistic as to finding anything at the locations depicted. Still, I thought it was a worthwhile project to pursue.

I should like to mention my true feeling here concerning Bill Jackson and his research material. When I first met Bill, he was four years older than me. In spite of this he was friendly towards me and always wanted to include me in his activities with George Porter, who was three years older than me. When I found that we both went to the same Church I began to look forward to seeing him there and we would hang out after the Sunday School period but before the Church Service that my mother always attended with my mentally disabled sister. We would usually go to Black's Stationary store to buy cigarettes, pipe tobacco, candy, etc.

I was sweet on Mr. Black's daughter Rachael, so we would converse occasionally. Bill often gave me advice on this situation that I appreciated being rather shy in that area. When he went to military service it left a void in my life. Then when he returned and was looking for work, I recommended he contact Dan Spartan whom I met upon the death of my girlfriend Yvette. Dan and I met at her funeral, and he had dated her prior to me. Bill worked for Dan while continuing his schooling to become a Doctor of Medicine.

Then Bill and George had a falling out concerning Bill's constant playing of one song every time we went out together. The song was The Irish Rover by Tommy Makin and the Clancy Brothers. When I got the two of them back together, they invited me to go with them fishing on the Hudson River in a sixteen-foot, inboard motorboat belonging to a friend of Bill's named Juan. Bill and George had both been certified as divers. I had not. They should not have agreed to let me experience diving in scuba gear and should not have left me alone on the bottom. George preceded me up to the surface and I rose hastily to catch up with him not watching where the boat had moved to. Thus, I came up under the idling propellor. It hit the regulator on the Scuba equipment and that hit the back of my head rendering me unconscious and I drowned. George saw this and got me to the surface while Bill and Juan got me on *the boat's deck and administered resuscitation procedures that brought me back to life. They thought I was dead for some four and one-half minutes but if the time in the water and getting me into the boat is included it was probably seven or eight minutes. Thus, I felt I owed them my life. George never asked anything of me but if I asked him, he obliged without question. Bill on the other hand, was always looking for company on his many excursions and I readily agreed to accompany him. After all he had saved my life. I felt obligated.*

As these excursions became more frequent and involved hiking, I readily agreed as this endeavor coincided with my plans to build up my stamina with the idea of emulating Mr. Colin Fletcher, a prolific author and hiker that wrote several books on the subject. I intended to walk the Arizona desert from Scottsdale to Payson and Pine, about the Mogollon Rim, and in the Grand Canyon as Mr. Fletcher had done and written about. In this endeavor I began to accompany Bill on his many excursions eventually becoming interested in why he was pursuing a particular course of hiking first in Newfoundland and Prince Edward Island then in the Adirondack Mountains of New York State and finally in the Catskills. As I questioned him, he was always vague and non-committal about what he was looking for and how he knew what to look for. This piqued my interest more and so I continued to accompany him on these trips eventually being caught up in his enthusiasm, and because he was the one that paid for them.

When he found the cave area, I helped him—because now I was interested enough to believe that he was actually correct in his assumptions. I thought the finding of the cave would be the culmination of his obsession, but it was just the beginning. However, I did not realize the extent of his research till his oldest son, Mark, gave me his "De Leon" file after Bill died.[22] This, however, was written by Mr. Denton Maier. He was the secretary of an amateur archaeology group Bill belonged to. This document, however, I came to learn had many inconsistencies and assumptions made by Denton. Bill died in 2000.

---

22 Bill Jackson and his friends in the archaeology club referred to the document he purchased as the "De Leon File." Don and Scott changed the name to the "Cremona Document."

Then in 2008, I discovered floppy disks behind the picture Bill had previously given to me when he and his family moved to Ireland. Once the information on them was presented to me I became fascinated with his material and began to ask his friends and associates if any of them had any material that was related to his research. Over time, I began to get material that has taken me up to the present.

With the material given me by Mrs. Lennon after the death of her husband, I shared this with Scott and Janet Wolter. Scott soon informed me via telephone that he had identified the island on the map as Campbell Island in the Cape Fear River of North Carolina and that it was privately owned. He said he would call the owners and I sarcastically replied, "Good luck with that." Still, Scott had been a successful television personality investigating odd occurrences and places on his show titled, America Unearthed. *I must admit I was surprised when he told me that the conversation with Ms. Madison Robideau, the representative for the Trask Family Trust, had been so well received. The only limiting factors were that the owners of the island, The Trask Family Trust, wanted the lion's share of any treasure found to which I did not object as I was skeptical we would actually find anything. Also, we were limited with a two-month time window in which to search the island. The Trasks did not want a continuing situation as was occurring on Oak Island in Nova Scotia by the Lagina Brothers. Thus, the dates chosen by Scott and Janet were in November of 2021. It would still be quite warm in North Carolina then.*

The Trask family would also provide boat transportation to and from the island and be available to participate in the search. To all of these arrangements I had no objection. However, the boat provided was smaller than I had anticipated and the trip caused some problems for me. I had a pinched sciatic nerve in the left portion of my back that made me a bit uncomfortable traveling the five miles from the landing to their island—a trip of about thirty-five minutes, at about 7 miles an hour—enduring bouncing over the river's swells and wave action from other passing boats, as well as the wind in my face—all this hurt my back and caused me to endure the otherwise enjoyable trip in some painful discomfort. This I failed to acknowledge to our hosts as I was not going to look a gift horse in the mouth, so to speak.

The first landing site was chosen for its proximity to the supposed location marked on one of the aerial photographs Bill Jackson had arranged to be taken of the island. In my opinion, it was less than ideal, and I wound up getting both feet and legs wet to get myself and the search materials out of the boat and onto the island. Scott was able to use his GPS application in his cellphone to locate the dig site easily however, and we began to shovel dirt into a screened sieve. I had previously been involved with this procedure during digs with the New York Archaeology Association, of whom I was a member. The soil was moist and required that it be rubbed through the screen to locate any artifacts contained in it. This was tiring work, but we shared turns doing this or digging.

After a break for lunch, Scott and the Trask family members continued this procedure. Janet continued to use the metal detector to locate any other metal locations outside the dig site. She was finding fishing weights, lures, bottle caps, pull tabs, and other detritus mostly within a few inches of the surface. Then she got a signal about ten feet to the left of the dig site but had trouble pinpointing it. She called me over, as I had a hand device called a pin-pointer. This was used by detectorists to locate finds. Mine located metal to within nine inches of the surface. I began to insert the probe into the sandy soil and was getting a signal but could not locate the object exactly. I asked her to shovel several scoops of dirt into the sieve so I could screen the soil through it in a further attempt to locate the elusive object.

When she had two good shovelfuls of sand in the sieve, I told her to put the metal detector into the area we just removed the sand from. Doing this the detector was silent indicating the metal object was now in the screen. I began to rub the sand through the screen till most of it was gone, still with no results till finally I felt something hard and flat. I handed it to Janet who cleaned it off and yelled to Scott and the others that we had found a coin! Further examination of it revealed, via an Internet search, that we had discovered a Dutch penny, slightly worn.

As it was after noon, so we now moved to the second site listed on Bill Jackson's pictures. This was more to the southern end of the island and required moving the boat and equipment to it. The second landing site was in a better, more open location. Scott got a strong signal here and everyone *believed we had found the box to which Bill had made the key to open. Digging began at a feverish pace. I was intrigued. After about eighteen inches, water came into the hole, but this was widened and digging continued. I, however, was in some pain as I had been standing or walking for most of the day and my back was hurting me badly. I stepped aside and took a pain medication while resting my butt on a fallen tree nearby.*

Scott had his hands into the water in the hole and had felt a straight metal surface that had an angle to it. Digging continued at a rapid pace while he continued to manipulate the underwater metal to get a firm grip on it. Finally, it came free revealing that it was a bent piece of steel some two feet long. There was no further positive signal from the metal detector and so we realized that we would have to settle for the penny as the only find of the trip. All I wanted to do was lay down on a soft bed and rest my aching back. Happily, the return trip by boat was against the wind though it was also against any river current. By the time we reached the dock and unloaded the equipment from the boat and put it into our vehicles I was really tired and sore.

When asked how we could split up the treasure find I told everyone that it belonged to the island's owner, represented by Mr. Webster Trask and his son, both of whom accompanied and helped in this endeavor. Mr. Kitchen, a Trask family relative and the provider of the second boat, was also part of this expedition whose invaluable help and interest was greatly appreciated. I slept like a rock that night.

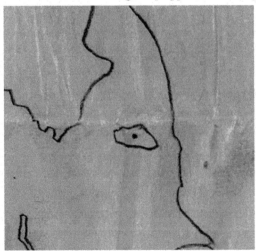

On the map Dr. Jackson traced in pencil in the early 1990s, the island where the cedar-lined treasure box was buried has an oval-shaped area that corresponds to one of the two aerial photographs marked with an "X" that were included in the wooden puzzle left for Don Ruh. Inside the oval-shaped area is a dot apparently marking the spot where the box was once buried. (Courtesy of Donald Ruh)

With regards to my association with Mrs. Janet Wolter, I found her to be a pleasant and attractive woman that was apparently very supportive of her husband's endeavors and was not afraid to get her hands dirty in pursuing them. She was also not above letting us know if she disagreed with our assumptions on any particular point in our pursuing Dr. Jackson's material.

Dan Spartan Call

My eyes were barely open upon hearing my phone vibrate on the nightstand on December 27, 2020. I grabbed the phone and saw it was Don Ruh calling. Don's gruff voice sounded excited as he explained the conversation, he had earlier that morning:

I woke up when my phone rang at 4:30 a.m. and it was our friend Dan Spartan. He called to tell me the failed knee replacement to his left leg was now infected and he is getting his leg amputated in February. I then told him about our trip to North Carolina looking for Bill Jackson's treasure on Campbell Island and the coin Janet and I found. This triggered a memory and Dan said about ten years ago he found a tube containing an animal skin hide that was moldy and smelled bad from the warm wet climate (Dan lived in Southeast Asia). Dan and his son decided to copy the maps drawn on the animal hide using a drafting table as light passed through the hide. Because the hide was 36" x 24" in size only half fit on the drafting table so they cut a large piece of paper in half, traced the maps onto the two pieces of paper and then taped it together. Because the hide was in such bad shape, they threw the hide away and put the paper copy inside the tube. Dan's son then put it into his safe.

Don then asked Dan if he would send the map as it could help us with the Cremona Document research. Dan said he would send the map the next time he saw his son who lived roughly 150 miles away. As has become almost routine in the past two years, hearing that Don would be getting new Cremona Document material from yet another colleague once again raised our excitement and anticipation level. Little did I know as I hung up the phone that three days later, Dan Spartan, and Map 8, would deliver the first of many surprises.

On New Year's Eve Day, Don called me early again and said, "Go check your email and call me back." Sensing something good, I hurriedly opened my email and clicked on Don's message that had a photo attached:

> Guess Who
> This arrived in today's mail from J. Masters, Bowling Green, Va.
> There is no letter or anything but this picture and one other. This one has an image I think you will find familiar.
> Don.

Sensing the photo was related to Don's call with Dan, I excitedly clicked on the picture. Don was right, I instantly recognized the Cape Fear River/ Campbell Island map Jackson had left for Don that led to our treasure hunt in North Carolina six weeks earlier. Everything was the same except there were two distinct additions that were not present on the map Bill Jackson had left for Don. The first were two words written within what was depicting the Cape Fear River, "Rio Jordan." A quick internet search of the Cape Fear River revealed it was previously named Rio Jordan by the Spanish in 1526. The second notable difference was at the dot placed inside the "eye of the angelfish", where Janet and Don found the Dutch coin on Campbell Island, there was a line leading from the dot outside the drawing to an open area of the map where there were five lines of French text. The letters were easily discernable and once plugged into Google Translate resulted in a startling and sobering revelation: *"It was deleted/suppressed in one thousand seven hundred ninety-four."*

In French, the word *suppri* can mean either "deleted" or "suppressed." To us, the word meant "recovered." The realization the treasure had apparently already been recovered was only a little disappointing. In fact, the treasure having already been recovered confirmed why we didn't find the eighteenth-century chest on Campbell Island, despite Don having the key. Even more significant—it boosted the importance of the Dutch coin we did find during the dig dated 1790. If the treasure had been recovered in 1794, the then 4-year-old coin could have been lost, or intentionally left, possibly as an offering, by a member of the party who recovered the treasure chest.

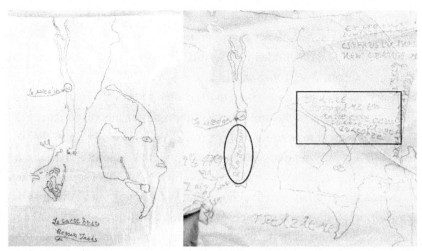

The map of Campbell Island and the Cape Fear River was copied by Dr. William Jackson from Map 8 of the Cremona Document, pictured at right. There are two important parts that appear on Map 8 not present on the Jackson copy. The first are the words, "Rio Jordan" (circled) which is what the Spanish named what is now the Cape Fear River, in 1526. The second is five lines of French text (boxed area) at the end of a line that extends from the "Eye of the Angelfish" where we found the Dutch coin dated 1790. Translated to English it reads, "It was deleted/suppressed in one thousand seven hundred ninety-four." Our interpretation was the treasure was recovered in 1794 meaning the 1790 coin could have been lost, or intentionally left as a token, likely by a member of the party who recovered the treasure box. (Courtesy of Donald Ruh)

If the 1790 coin was connected to the recovery of the treasure, it suddenly became vitally important in confirming the veracity of the Cremona Document, that treasures had been placed on numerous islands, and in this case, to pay Lafayette for his service during the America Revolution.

Later that day, Don sent another email that arrived with another picture taken by Dan Spartan of Map 8. This picture showed a different area on the map that included parts of five familiar maps and one Scott didn't recognize. The five maps he recognized were what we have come to call the "South Wall Map in Jerusalem", "Cape Cod", "Narragansett Bay", "Nova Scotia", and the "Dragon and the Lamb". The map he didn't recognize looked like a corkscrew at first glance, but then it dawned on him, this was a detailed drawing of the six Templar knights' exploration of the tunnel system and chamber under the South Wall. Upon this realization, I grabbed my latest book, *Cryptic Code of the Templars in America: Origins of the Hooked X™*, turned to page 177 and started rereading the narrative.

With each passage it became clear whoever made the original sketch chronicled every detail. I was amazed to read about, and then see, where they broke through the wall and entered the tunnel system, where they encountered the spring clearly drawn on the map, the two sets of stairs they walked down, and the hidden pit "Bernrd" fell part way into that was lined with steel spikes. Everything was captured in the drawing with incredible accuracy including the description of the contents inside the secret chamber after the six knights broke through the timbers protecting the entrance.

This is a good time to remind the reader that in the Martinist Templar tradition, this early twelfth-century mission into the catacombs beneath the Temple Mount in Jerusalem was not a blind search of discovery. These men knew exactly what they were looking for, and where they would find it as the information of this secret chamber was passed down through the Tradition for centuries beginning in the first century AD. Conventional history says the Templars were driven out of the Holy Land by the Muslims led by Saladin in 1187. This is a myth, as by that time the order had completed its mission of rounding up important relics, documents, technology and of course, gold, and other wealth in the Middle and Near East, as well as Egypt. What many historians call a retreat was an intentional withdrawal from their headquarters on the Temple Mount for the simple reason that their mission based in Jerusalem was completed. The treasures they accumulated were then split up and taken west eventually bringing that wealth to the "Western Lands" with the goal of founding the New Jerusalem in North America. That sacred mission is chronicled in incredible detail in the Sinclair/Wemyss journals, and the Cremona Document, and was known within the Tradition as the Covenant. However, that sacred agreement with Deity was not made in His name, it was made in honor of the sacred feminine they referred to as the Great Goddess.

Once the Templar knights had cut through the timbers, they entered the ritual chamber carved in the sacred 2:1 ratio of an oblong square. This room, with a hole cut into the roof extending far above them, they concluded was, "an early Christian meeting place." It contained what they believed was an Ivri (Jewish) sacrificial altar in the east end of the chamber. The drawing even shows "...*a groove at one end and a hollow in its center.*" The four ossuaries are drawn in a rectangular arrangement and the fish on the floor made with ceramic tiles includes an easily discernable eye in the drawing. The cistern is drawn on the west side of the chamber with the wavy lines representing the flowing spring, most likely the intermittent Gihon spring. The

Cremona Document narrative says the crusaders encountered this spring shortly after entering the tunnel system under the South Wall. The level of detail depicted in the drawing was extraordinary and adds credibility to this important aspect of the Cremona Document story.

Scanning the photo, I noticed something near the Cape Cod Map that looked familiar. Upon magnifying the picture, I could see the sigil of the scribe who appears to have copied the maps and wrote the two pages of notes and comments in multiple languages. This three-letter symbol looked different than the other examples and prompted much thought as to who this person might have been. The answer to the question turned out to be on the first photo Don received. Directly above the commentary in French that delivered the news about the Campbell Island treasure, were four more lines of text that tuned out to be written in Latin. Translated into English it produced the following:

"*According to your will, Tudicus, the job it is to itemize. Clyphus Lucinus Yzerbo 17. New Orange MDCXLIII (1663).*"

It would be another day before Don sent the other two pictures, one of which was an overall view of most of Map 8. This picture showed the group of four lines of Latin that was in the upper center of the map suggesting the comment referred to the scribe who drew the copies of the Cremona Document. What excited us most was what appeared to be the name of the man behind the mysterious CLY siglum, Clyphus Lucinus Yzerbo. The Roman numeral seventeen (XVII) after the name could indicate he was the seventeenth generation carrying the family name, but it wasn't clear. What is clear, and important, is a Google search of the name produced nothing. The point is, if we could find this name on the internet, then a hoaxer could too. Since we did not, this fact serves to bolster the veracity of Map 8, and by association it bolsters the authenticity of the entire document.

New Orange with a date of 1663 (MDCXVIII) is written below the Clyphus name. What does this mean? What we do know is New York City was settled by the Dutch Republic and named New Amsterdam in 1624. In 1664, the British took the city over and renamed it New York City. This lasted until 1673 when the Dutch retook the city naming it New Orange. It is unclear if this is what Map 8 is referring to, but what is relevant is the Dutch

East India Company was based in New Amsterdam/New Orange and it was they who minted the 1790 coin found on Campbell Island.

In Bill Jackson's narrative, he speculated if De Sudeley brought back evidence in the form of documents, and specifically the marriage document of Jesus and Mary Magdalene, they would have had powerful leverage over the Church and provide incentive for why they were eventually put down in 1307.

The four pictures of the various parts of Map 8 had us itching with anticipation to see the actual map Dan Spartan had promised to send to Don. It seemed that even during the Covid-19 pandemic, with all its challenges for us personally and for people around the world, there was a lot to look forward to in the new year of 2021. It was indeed a fantastic year for the Cremona Document, and the Sinclair/Wemyss Journals, that provided exciting new revelations about the Templars in America.

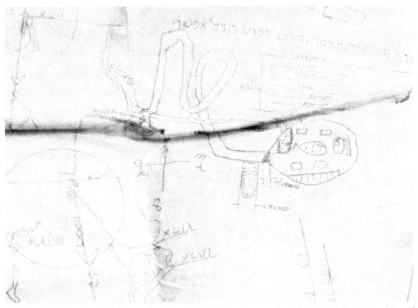

This is a cropped image of the second picture of Map 8 Dan Spartan emailed to Don Ruh in December of 2020. It shows parts of the Cape Cod, Narragansett Bay and Nova Scotia maps, as well as a detailed drawing of the tunnel/cave system the Templars used to locate a hidden ritual chamber under the South Wall in Jerusalem. (Courtesy of Donald Ruh)

CHAPTER 7:

DRAGON AND THE LAMB

Learning about how some of the Templar treasure was used to pay General Marquis de Lafayette for his service in the Revolutionary War was a very pleasant surprise. However, that wasn't the only fascinating revelation to be learned about what the long-hidden treasures were used for. We also learned about what happened to one of two treasures Earl Henry Sinclair buried on Dog Island after his ship, the *Catherine*, became hopelessly stranded after being blown onto the island in a horrific storm in 1398.

On February 4, 2018, John Drake died after complications from a stroke he suffered on December 24, 2017, triggering the release to Don of the Cremona materials that were Drake's possession thanks to Bill Jackson.

Dr. Jackson passed away in 2000 and in the past twenty-three years, several of those colleagues who received parts of the document have also passed on. I have been very fortunate to have been present when Don opened some of these packages, which were always delivered in a clever way, but the delivery of the document he received from Dr. Jackson via John Drake's estate on October 13, 2018, was not only very clever, but entertaining as well.

Janet and I arrived at Don's home with two close friends, and he greeted us with a big toothy smile. *"Come on in."* he said, and we excitedly entered his home. After the Janet and I introduced our friends, Jason and Holly, Don gestured to a small table with a wooden box sitting on it that was covered with wooden fish. Don then said with a slight laugh, "This is what I got from my friend John Drake. It's a fish box that's actually a puzzle I had to figure out how to open."

I pulled out my phone and recorded Don's explanation of how he figured out how to open the box. In short, the number of fishes of the sides of the box were the numbers Don had to put in sequence on dials inside the box that were revealed after he opened the front side by moving one of the fish on the box. Once he entered the proper sequence of numbers, the right side of the box slid out revealing a hidden door with the Latin Phrase painted on it: *In Hoc Signo Vince* (In This Sign, Thou Shall Conquer).

True to form, Don had already opened the compartment and shared with them what he found. The compartment contained a plastic bag with pictures, a strange medallion with a skull on the top, and a letter from his friend dated December 25, 2016, explaining the purpose of the fish box, which was a treasure hunt Drake had left for Don to find. Drake's letter also confirmed what Don had always told me, that Dr. Jackson had sold the Cremona Document to the notorious Vatican Archbishop, Paul Marcinkus.

The wooden fish box Donald Ruh received from the estate of his deceased friend John Drake. After figuring out how to open it, he found instructions to find a modest treasure his friend had buried for Don to find, and what appeared to be a late Eighteenth Century letter with a map on the back. (Wolter, 2018)

THIS DEVICE IS ALSO . . . TO BE A **ONE TIME PAD**
. When the proper combination is acquired write it with the letters A, B, C, D, E, F over them.
Each wheel has numbers from 0 to 9. Set the number under C first, then follow with E, A, D, B, F.
F controls the internal door lock. A receding plug at P indicates the door is locked, an advancing
Plug open. Remove the steel rod and connecter from L and stab its end through the upper eye.
Place side of rod at X and push connecter left while turning yellow left fish till black line is
Parallel with the right side. Left side should slide free. If not YOU ARE FUCKED.-J. D.

Once Don removed the front side wooden panel it revealed six dials of a combination lock and the following instructions taped to the panel. (Courtesy of Donald Ruh)

Once Don had figured out how to open the front and right side of the Fish box, a wooden door covering a secret compartment was exposed and it had a Christian cross and the Latin words, "In Hoc Signo Vince", painted on it which means "In this Sign, Thou Shall Conquer." (Wolter, 2018)

Also in the compartment, was a small metal box containing a picture and another small wooden box that contained pictures with clues to the hidden treasure. Don also found a small book, which I recognized as a Masonic cipher book, which had clues hidden within the pages in invisible ink—for locating Drake's treasure.

After explaining how he opened the fish box, he showed us the treasure he had already found: rare coins and rolls of pennies inside an ammunitions box. Don also found a small, black-colored cylinder inside the compartment which he had waited for our arrival to open. The wooden end-cap Don pulled off to open the cylinder was adorned with a beautiful metal medallion of a Jerusalem Cross with a profile of Jesus in the center. I remember wondering if this medallion was placed by a Freemason or a Roman Christian? While the two aren't necessarily mutually exclusive, a deeply initiated and spiritual Freemason most likely would not be Roman Catholic.

With my cell phone camera rolling again, I filmed as Don pulled the wooden cap off and poured out the items that had been rattling inside the tube. What landed

December 25, 2016

Dear Don

Bill wanted you to have the note, map on the back, and entrusted it to Dan and I. He thought and we concurred that you were the best person to follow this up if there was anything to still follow up. Bill did not want Bishop Marcinkus to have this.

Sam Wright's son in law's uncle made the box we call a "FISH BOX" and we used it for this purpose as well as the following.

There is still a little money in my portion of the Spartan account plus some stuff that belonged to Cathy and some pennies I collected over the years as you have. I have secured them in New York and the location is shown here. Both Dan and I thought you should have another Treasure Hunt especially after the business with the PUZZLE TABLE. Have fun. We have no doubt you will be able to solve the puzzle but you should keep in mind that the inference provided by the boxes ornamentation may have nothing to do with either treasure location.

I have always admired your work with us in Spartan Enterprises and fully understand your motivation in being engaged in that work. I am also thoroughly thankful for your introduction to my wife Cathy. She has made my life worth living. Her passing has left a hole in my heart and my life that neither my two beautiful daughters nor our grandchildren can fill.
Your continued friendship over the years and your recent help with Hank's daughter's problem that resulted in your injury has greatly affected my appreciation of you. I hope that you will continue to enjoy your retirement and will have a long and happy life.

Your friend
Sincerely,

John

One of the items inside the fish box was a letter written to Donald Ruh by his recently deceased friend, John Drake. The letter explains the contents of the box and confirms the story that Dr. Jackson sold the Cremona Document to the notorious Vatican Archbishop, Paul Marcinkus. (Courtesy of Donald Ruh)

Don Ruh shared the treasure his friend John Drake left for him to find in his will. (This page) The wooden end cap of the cylinder hidden inside the fish box had a medallion of a stylized Jerusalem Cross with Alpha-Omega symbols and a profile of Jesus at the center. (Opposite) Inside the metal ammunition box was jewelry, various rare coins, and rolls of wheat pennies both men collected.
(Wolter, 2018/2018)

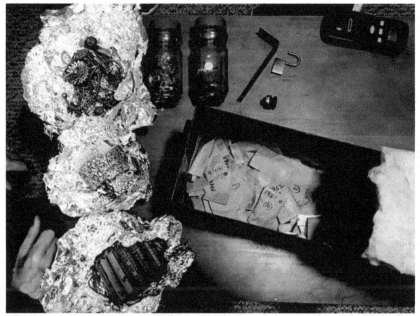

on the table were four small stones, two of which were Herkimer diamonds,[23] a piece of coal, a small flake of gray chert, what looked like a small highly weathered coin, a piece of metal, and a small gold-colored pendant with Jesus on one side and Mary with child on the other. Why these items were inside the tube was lost on Don and everyone else, but the last item in the tube was fully understood by all.

Don carefully removed the remining item with tweezers that looked to be inside old wrapping paper as he slid it out. Once removed, Don carefully unwrapped the delicate brown paper to reveal another old, yellowed piece of paper with writing on it. We all realized it was a letter, hand-written in French, with three easily discernable dates, 1422, and 1749 twice, suggesting the letter was written sometime after 1749. When turned over, there was a map of what looked like multiple islands with three small dots next to more French text below the drawings. The letter written by John Drake made it clear this was another part Dr. Jackson had pulled from the Cremona Document which he wanted Don to have. Upon closer inspection, the reason the letter was pulled by Jackson was because it was a map apparently marking the location of at least two treasure sites.

---

23 Double-terminated quartz crystals only found in exposed outcrops of dolomite in and around Herkimer County, New York, and the Mohawk River Valley in the US. https://en.wikipedia.org/wiki/Herkimer_diamond

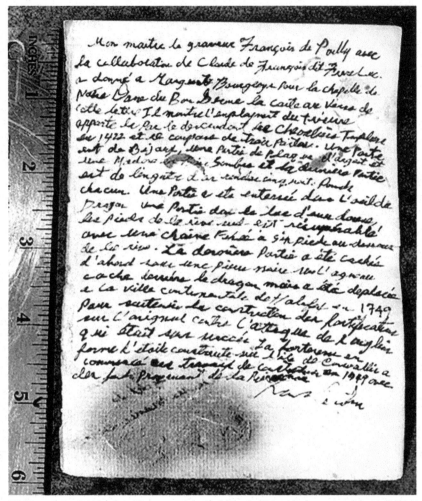

The letter written in French, with a map on the back, was inside a cylinder retrieved from a hidden compartment within a wooden "Fish Box" made by friends and bequeathed to Don Ruh by John Drake's estate after his death on February 4, 2018. (Wolter, 2018)

At this point, there were two things that needed to be done. The first was to get the handwritten French translated into English, and the second was to determine where these islands were. Logic told us these treasures had most likely already been recovered. However, we also knew there was only one way to find out! Getting the translations done turned out to be relatively easy. The first person we reached out to was our close friend and then current Supreme Grand Master of Knights Templar in Canada, William

"Bill" Mann. Bill forwarded a copy of the letter to his sister Cheryl, who was a recently retired college professor with a PhD in language who speaks six different languages including French.

On August 17, 2020, in a conference call with Bill, Cheryl, Janet, and myself, Cheryl read her translation and then emailed it a few days later. Her comments in brackets indicate some hesitation with the translation:

> My master the engraver François de Poilly, with the collaboration
> of Claude de François, dit Brother Luc, gave to Marguerite Bourgeoys
> for the chapel of Notre-Dame du Bon Secuors, the map at the reverse of
> this letter. He shows the employment of the [treasure] brought there by
> the descendant of Chevalier Templars in 1422 and it is compose[d] of
> three parts. One part is jewelry. One part of silver plate and a Madonna
> with a somber smile and the last part is ingots of gold rendering [worth]
> 50 pounds each. One part was entered in the eye of the Dragon. One
> part in the lake [d'aux douse les pieds-twelve feet] from the south shore—
> is recoverable with a fixed chain six feet below the shore. The last part
> was first hidden under a black stone a lamb hidden behind the dragon
> but was moved to the continental city of Halifax in 1749 to support the
> construction of the fortifications on [the original] against the attack of
> the English which was without success. The fortress constructed in the
> form of a star at the word of Cornwallis began the work of construction
> in 1749 with [fonds provenant] funds coming from [?Rein...].

The second person we reached out to, was another Freemason who lived in Phoenix, Arizona, Edward Ronstadt-Martinez, PhD. Several years earlier while at a gathering at his home Brother Ed introduced Janet and I, to another Freemason named Andre' Salmon, 33-degree of the Scottish Rite, who is both an academic and a professional linguist, and retired from the World Bank who was born in France with dual citizenship and fluent in the language. On August 18, 2020, Ed emailed Andre's translation:

> My master, the engraver François de Poilly in collaboration with
> Claude de François, known as Brother Luc, gave Marguerite Bourgeoys for
> the chapel of Notre-Dame du Bon [Secuors] [...illegible...] the map at the
> back of this letter. He shows the location of the treasure brought there by

the descendant of Knights Templar of 1422 and is composed of three parts. One part is jewels. One part is a silver plaque and a black stone Madonna. And the last part is gold ingots worth fifty pounds each. One part has been buried in the eye of the Dragon. One part in the lake [...illegible...] at the feet of the southeastern shore is recoverable with a chain attached six feet below the shore. The last part had been hidden at first under a black stone on the lamb hidden behind the dragon but was moved to the continental city of Halifax in 1749 to support construction of fortifications on the Moose River against the attack of the English which was unsuccessful. The star-shaped fortress built on Cornwallis Island started the construction work in 1749 with funds originating from the Renaissance.

As one can see the translations are nearly identical and the information conveyed is clear. François de Poilly (1623-1693) was a seventeenth century French engraver who at some point, most likely in France, met with Marguerite Bourgeoys (1620-1700) and gave her the map marking the location of three separate treasures brought to Nova Scotia in 1422. Like the treasures brought over by Earl Henry Sinclair just twenty-four years earlier in 1398, these treasures apparently joined the two treasures already buried by Earl Henry and his men on what was then called Dog Island. It was later named Cornwallis Island, after Edward Cornwallis (1713-1776), the first Governor of Nova Scotia, and is now called McNabs Island. McNabs Island is being referred to as the "Dragon" in the letter with the "Lamb" being Lawlor Island to the northeast.

At first glance, when the shapes of the islands drawn on the back of the letter are compared with modern maps, they don't look at all the same. However, upon closer inspection of the specific geographic features and the two islands' relative position to each other, it becomes obvious these are the two islands being depicted. It is also likely the person drawing the maps intentionally exaggerated the features of McNab Island to veil its identity which would have been effective in the Eighteenth Century when high qual-ity, detailed maps of Nova Scotia, and Google Earth, didn't exist.

Our expert translators agree the letter was written by the French Catholic Priest and missionary, Jean-Louis Le Loutre (1709-1772). When researching him it becomes clear, he was not a supporter of British aggression in Nova Scotia at the time and became leader of the French, Acadian, and Mi'kmaq militias fighting

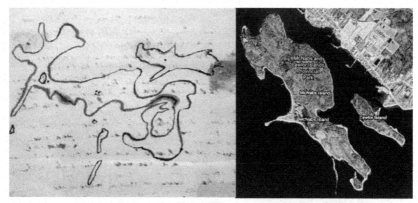

When comparing the two islands drawn on the back of the letter written by the French Catholic Priest Jean-Louis Le Loutre, with modern maps they don't look much alike. However, when comparing detailed geographic features, it becomes clear they are in fact, McNab and Lawlor Islands. (Courtesy of Donald Ruh, Internet)

the King's army in Nova Scotia then called Acadia. Le Loutre first arrived in Nova Scotia in 1738 and after leading revolts and numerous battles and skirmishes that failed to wrest control of Acadia from the British, he realized he was a marked man and boarded a ship for France in 1755. The ship was seized, Le Loutre was captured and imprisoned for eight years until his release in 1763. While it is possible Le Loutre could have written the letter sometime after 1763 until his death 1772, it seems more likely it was written between 1749 and 1755.

One of the biggest problems of the Le Loutre letter, is we don't know the timing of critical events mentioned, such as when it was written, and when the map was given to Marguerite Bourgeoys who began the effort to build a chapel in 1655.[24] It appears the map given to her was for the purpose of recovering the treasure to finance the building of Notre-Dame du Bon Secuors. This seemed like a noble effort by Bourgeoys to build the first Marion (religious buildings dedicated to the Virgin Mary) pilgrimage church in Ville-Marie (Montreal), but was there an ulterior motive to Marguerite's efforts? Based on a different letter Don Ruh received in May of 2017, the answer appears to be yes!

In my previous book, *Cryptic Code of the Templars in America: Origins of the Hooked X™*, on pages 275-281 I discussed the Lionel De Walderne 21st letter Don received in April of 2017, concluding the First Century scrolls remaining at the Temple of the Goddess on Hunter Mountain were collected and, *"Have gotten a missive from Father Olier to go to his place of the Sulpicians to the north,*

---

24 https://margueritebourgeoys.org/en/marguerite-bourgeoys/

(7-10) Jean-Louis Le Loutre (1709-1772) was a French Catholic Priest and Missionary who led French, Acadian, and Mi'kmaq militia groups against the British that were ultimately unsuccessful. He was captured and imprisoned in 1755 until his release in 1763. When he wrote the letter with the treasure maps is unknown but is believed to have been sometime between 1749 and 1755 or as late as 1772, when he died. (Internet)

beyond the great north river." That place was what is now Montreal.

By the time of the writing of Lionel De Walderne 21's letter on May 8, 1656, the scrolls had already been recovered and likely made their way north to Montreal. Could it be that Marguerite Bourgeoys knew of the cache of highly valuable and religiously controversial scrolls and was doing her part to create a repository to house them? The timing seems to work perfectly as the first stone for the foundation of Notre Dame de Bon Secours church was laid that same year in 1656.[25] While construction of the church would be delayed and not completed until 1675, the plan to create the perfect hiding place with some of the treasure from McNabs (the Dragon) and Lawlor (the Lamb) Islands begins to make more sense.

There is no question the people mentioned in the letter, and Le Loutre himself, were connected by knowledge of the descendants of the Knights Templar who buried treasures in North America for future use in founding what they considered the biblical prophecy of the New Jerusalem. While outwardly Catholic, they all clandestinely embraced a different view of the story of the First Century Royal Family and worked to further the goals and obligations of the Venus Families the Templars had passed onto them. Information was passed on to members of secret societies that in this case was likely the *Compagnie du Saint-Sacrement* (Company of the Blessed Sacrament) which was founded in 1630.[26] Hostility plagued the society

25 Bernier, Page 160, 2001.
26https://www.encyclopedia.com/religion/encyclopedias-almanacs-tran-

The sketch of Francois de Poilly (the elder) was drawn by Jean Louis Roullet in 1699, six years after the subject's death. Poilly passed the map of what are veiled depictions of McNabs and Lawlor Islands in Nova Scotia, Canada, to French nun Saint Marguerite Bourgeoys, for the Church of Notre Dame de Bon Secours in Montreal, Canada. These French nationalists must have been members of a Rosicrucian related order to have such vitally important information about Templar treasure in North America. The stain glass depiction of Marguerite Bourgeoys teaching children is from the Notre Dame Basilica in Montreal, Canada. (Internet, Wolter, 2022)

beginning in 1660 and it was dissolved by 1666. While it was the end of this secret society, disbanded members were initiated into other orders with Templar secrets and the same long-range agenda, like the Rosicrucian's, and continued.[27] Half a century later, another group with intimate knowledge of clandestine Templar activities in the North America was officially founded by the Grand Lodge of England in 1717 and was called Freemasonry.[28,29]

There are a couple of important takeaways from Jean-Louis Le Loutre's letter with the maps. First, is the mention of treasure brought, *"...by the descendant of Knights Templar of/in 1422."* This was twenty-four years after Earl Henry Sinclair's last visit to North America and since there is no mention in the Sinclair/Wemyss journals of a trip to the Western lands in

scripts-and-maps/compagnie-du-saint-sacrement
27 https://www.rosicrucian.org/
28 https://www.freemason.com/how-to-join/what-is-freemasonry/
29 https://www.nationalgalleries.org/art-and-artists/42969/francois-de-poilly-elder-1623-1693-french-engraver

1422, this must be a different faction of Knights Templars from somewhere other than Scotland. This is easy to believe as it is well known factions of the order survived after their official dissolution in 1307. The most well-known is the Order of Christ in Portugal that remained an official order until 1835. It is reasonable to assume the leadership of the surviving Templar groups in Europe and Scandinavia maintained communication and coordination of the long-range grand plan of establishing a sanctuary they called "New Jerusalem", in North America. From where this specific Templar order originated is unknown. However, given the key players in the letter and those who were in Montreal at the time of its founding were all French, it's a safe bet the Templars who brought these treasures likely originated in France. What emerges from this letter and the other documents is a cohesive and consistent story that historians can no longer ignore.

Another interesting thing in the letter is the symbolic use of the "dragon" and the "lamb" for McNabs and Lawlor Islands. Lawlor Island as the 'lamb' works as it is the significantly smaller of the two islands that symbolically like the followers of a priest in a congregation, or "sheep", the island is dwarfed in size and relative importance by the larger one. The use of the word "dragon" takes a little more investigation to put into proper context. Given Jean-Louis Le Loutre was initiated and understood the true history of the Essene tradition, he was likely referring to the biblical passage in the *Book of Revelation 12*, about the dragon, the woman, and child. The dragon represents evil or the devil, that was often depicted on old maps as a dragon serpent of the sea. Incredibly, an artifact discovered in 1945 provided important evidence to explain the symbolism of the dragon. Where was this found? At Notre Dame de Bon Secours.

As I wrote about in *Akhenaten to the Found Fathers: Mysteries of the Hooked X™*, Janet and I traveled in October of 2009 to Montreal with our friends, David and Kim Brody. We made several enlightening discoveries which I shared in my book, including many photographs. One of the items photographed in the basement of Bon Secours Church was a copper printing plate that was found with a foundation stone. The image on the plate is Madonna and a child, standing on a crescent with a dragon under her feet. Why the dragon and what does it mean? Canadian author Francine Bernier wrote about the plate explaining how it was placed with the foundation stone by benefactor Pierre Chevrier de Fancamp as the plate is also has his family Coat of Arms.

(Left) During a trip to Montreal in October of 2009, Scott took a picture of a metal printing plate of a Madonna and child, standing on a crescent and dragon that was excavated in the foundation of the original church of Notre Dame de Bon Secours. (Right) The octagonal copper base of the steeple at Notre Dame de Bon Secours Chapel looks strikingly like the Newport Tower in Newport, Rhode Island, and the altars of Knights Templar Chapels around in Europe (see Foreword). (Wolter, 2009/2009)

Bernier makes the argument that the vanquished dragon below the Lady's feet has a more esoteric symbolic meaning. That she is not the Virgin and baby Jesus, but rather the Lady of the Apocalypse in the *Book of Revelation* (12: 1-9) attributed to John. Quoting Bernier, *"She wears the twelve-star crown—the Christian symbol of the Chosen People, also the Elect of the apocalyptic New Jerusalem in the Bible."*

The symbolic reference to the New Jerusalem is no coincidence as the underlying mission in these Templar/Masonic documents is the establishment of a New Jerusalem in North America. Bernier continues, *"...Fancamp's medal clearly associates this Lady with Stella Maris, "the venerable Virgin" who protects the pilgrims "crossing the tumultuous seas", which support the Chapel's name, Notre Dame de Bon Secours (Our Lady of Good Hope)."*

The appropriate symbolism of the Goddess protecting pilgrims crossing the ocean seeking the New Jerusalem from the 'serpent of the sea' (the dragon) could not be more appropriate for the brave souls who immigrated to the Montreal at the time of its founding.

Finally, in fact we have yet another independent, direct statement in an authentic Eighteenth-Century document about pre-Columbian descendants of the fugitive Knights Templar order, in the early Fifteenth Century in this case, bringing treasures from Europe to North America to be used for a future purpose. This powerful document adds to the already conclusive argument about the central role the medieval Knights Templar and their descendants, and later Rosicrucians and Freemasons, played in the founding of the United States of America.

CHAPTER 8:

ROBERTA'S DOCUMENT TROVE

This next chapter contains highly detailed information about what happened on Oak Island beginning in the late 14th century through the late 18th century. How this information came to Don was quite a shock, as we believed there weren't going to be anymore materials coming since all of the colleagues that Bill Jackson was thought to have given material to had died. Don is the last man standing and we were both sure that what we call the Dave Rian Cryptogram, which appeared the previous summer, was it. As fate would have it, we couldn't have been more wrong. Sadly, Roberta passed away in August of 2023. She requested privacy about her identity and location, and so we will respect her wishes and leave out certain details. What we can say is that Bill Jackson had a close friend, Iudea, who Don never met. When Iudea passed away in 2019, she left a cache of documents, maps, and sketches from Bill to her stepsister, Roberta. Through a mutual friend Don and Roberta were connected. In January of 2023, this person traveled to meet with Roberta to retrieve the remaining material Bill Jackson had given to Iudea.

Before diving in, let's back up to a conversation Don, Janet, and I had late one night in a hotel after an exhausting day in the woods looking for, and finding, treasure which we were led to by one of the Cremona Document maps. After cleaning and examining the artifacts we had discovered earlier in the day, I turned the topic to whether there could be anyone else still living that Bill Jackson could have given material to that could still make its way to Don at some point. He pondered the question and quickly concluded there was only one still-living individual from among their colleagues saying, "Bill and [this individual] did not get along and I doubt Bill would have left anything with him." Don then thought a moment longer and said, "There is one person who might still be living, who was a very good friend of Bill's. He may have given material to her, but she didn't work for the company."

Don said he'd follow up on the possible lead, and roughly five months later his digging and diligence paid off. It turned out an acquaintance of Don's recognized the name as a friend she graduated from college with in the early 1960's. Her name was Roberta, and Don's acquaintance reached out to the now 81-year-old woman who was recovering from a recent stroke. We were both a little nervous wondering if Roberta would reject us, but her response to Don's acquaintance was welcome news to all of us. She said she did have material Bill had given to Iduea and said she'd look for it.

MESSAGE #1

In early January of 2023, Don called saying he'd received a card from Roberta and inside were two pieces of paper. The first sheet contained drawings of two maps with strange symbols in various places on the page.

The second page was filled with rows of strange symbols on both sides that Don concluded were part of a twenty-six-character alphabet that looked like Greek symbols. As had become our routine, Janet and I made our way to New York to see Don as quickly as we could get there. On January 15, 2023, they arrived at Don's home and immediately went to work helping him decipher the message. Don had made good headway prior to their arrival and after three hours working together, they came up with a decrypted message that did not disappoint:

> *The power of God is within you. This is the final writing of this report.*
> *First done in MCCCVIII [1308] and revised three times till MCMVIII*
> *[1908]. The final putting of the relic is told here MDXCVII [1597]. In*
> *MCCCIV [1304] Louis de Grimoard by order of Grand Master Jaques*
> *DeMolay ar[r]anged for three ships to embark from LaRochelle to locale*
> *de [of] Ramsey and Point de [of] Arye and Leith de [of] Saddel dans [in]*

le [the] (Isle?) *de* [of] *Man with the pilot* (navigator?) *Francisco DeLeon, they embark to Harris West Isle for designer [architect?] Paolette Justinian Roach. Set sail Mars* [March] *XXI* [21] *for the brethren in northren* [Northern] *the northland. This is the account of the journey and the CCC* [300] *year project to secure the relic now held by Lionel de Waldern 111* [3rd] *XLIV* [44] *years old abo*[a]*rd le* [the] *Gaspard also captioned by Philip d' Armon with a crew of LVI* [56] *and I* [one] *chest of jewels and Jewelry with the relic. Philip d' Armont, relative of Pierre in Lo Tutore* [Italian: The Guardian] *with a crew of LXXIV* [74] *and III* [3] *chests of gold and silver bars. He also carries Ibrahim Muhammad Al-Zacara, maker of structure. Captain Juan de Alvarez from Garda Portugal in Le Vallant with chart maker Sotomon Yzarbo son of Licinius and a crew of LXVIII* [68] *with V* [5] *chests of gold and silver coin completes the trio. They ar*[r]*ive at the observatory in Juin* [June] *XXI* [21] *and leave Jillet* [July] *XXI* [21] *for the land of the Wasuta and the Mickimacks.*

It took us a few days to sit with and absorb this incredible message, it was a lot to wrap our heads around that all was being conveyed. Don and I do a much deeper dive interpreting this message in our other book but for this story it tells us important historical information that was previously unknown to the world.

It confirms the Knights Templar were successful in escaping France with their massive treasures prior to their suppression on October 13, 1307. Grand Master Jacques DeMolay anticipated trouble and ordered three ships loaded with treasure, and the "relic", to sail first to the Isle of Man and arrive at three different ports—so as not to lose all three ships and their precious cargo—should agents of the Church and the King of France be waiting at one of the ports. From there they likely sailed to Scotland, perhaps to hide the treasures in Kings Cave on the remote Island of Arran, and then eventually to Wemyss Caves on the north coast of the Firth of Forth before being brought to the "Western Lands" in 1395 and 1398.

Besides the many names of individuals and ships involved in the mission and details about the treasures they brought with them, we learn who the likely "designer" (architect) and "...maker of structure..." (engineer) of the "observatory" is, which can only mean the Newport Tower. I have repeatedly made the case that the Newport Tower was constructed by the ideological descendants of the Knights Templar circa 1400 AD and this document provides additional supporting evidence this conclusion is true. But let's get back to the new documents from Roberta and their connection to Oak Island.

The second page with the sketch and symbols has what we both believe is a rather crude drawing of Oak Island. The sketch actually contains considerable details that are consistent with the pervasive legend.

This page and opposite: The first encrypted message Don received from Roberta comprised two pages of strange symbols within a boxed grid system comprised of 24 columns and a total of 44 rows. The symbols comprised a 26-letter alphabet of Greek-like characters Don, thankfully, had seen before. (Courtesy of Donald Ruh)

First, there are three circles—which represent wells. The second of two circles on the western section of the island are labeled "well." The third circle has two lines running east to the ocean where it fans into four parts of what appears to be a drainage system. This well is in the general location of the eastern section of the island of what is famously known as the Money Pit. Between the two sections of the island in the area now called the "Swamp",

Lastly, the same message mentions a forge for making lime to fortify the stone structures used to build the underground workings of what they called, "The Underground Project."

At the time Don received the first two pages from Roberta, she sent word back she had more material from Bill Jackson including three pages that she said looked like original documents, not copies. More than a month later, on February 21, 2023, an envelope arrived at Janet and my residence with more than twenty pages of documents, including four more encrypted messages and three detailed sketches. Two weeks later, on March 11, 2023, Don received his copies of the messages and three original sketches on slightly yellowing paper. I immediately went to work deciphering the four messages, each one encrypted differently. It took three weeks to finish the work and the messages didn't disappoint. As stated earlier, we will focus on the parts of the messages that deal specifically with Oak Island. Information relevant to our forthcoming book, and not the Oak Island story, is redacted.

The second of two pages Don received from Roberta contains strange symbols and a crude map of Oak Island with separate drawings of what appear to be entrances to a subterranean tunnel system. The map also appears to show three well entrances as small circles, a forge, ████████████████, a boulder pavement running east-west across on the eastern section of the island and a drainage system into the ocean leading from the easternmost well entrance otherwise known as the "Money Pit." (Courtesy of Donald Ruh)

MESSAGE #2

The second of the five encrypted messages was comprised of a single page with rows of numbers in a box grid system labeled 10, and appeared to be an explanation about the underground workings of the tunnel system on Oak Island:

After deciphering and reading the message it quickly became apparent that one of the three pages of sketches was a detailed drawing of the underground tunnel system. It also dawned on us that we now knew the intricate details of the Templars subterranean activities on Oak Island and how badly the Lagina brothers would want this information to use on *The Curse of Oak Island*. Little did we know, there was a lot more to come.

MESSAGE #3

The third message we decoded was labeled "1000 & 2000" and was comprised of three pages of now familiar symbols within a grid system aligned into horizontal and vertical rows like the first message. The symbols were the same as those used for the numbers 0-9 in the Sacandaga Lake cryptogram. This time however, the symbols were used to make numbers 1-26 that corresponded to the twenty-six letters of the alphabet. The message that unfolded raised our eyebrows—we were learning details about exactly what happened to the treasure hidden on Oak Island in 1395, incredibly, after 374 years:

The second cryptogram Don received from Roberta was a page with symbols within a boxed grid system made of 24 columns and 25 rows. The encryption used a relatively simple number-to-letter alphabet that when decoded, revealed information about the tunnel system under Oak Island. (Courtesy of Donald Ruh)

In MDCCLXIX [1769] Capt'n Timothy MaClarin landed on the seaward side of the small island. He saw it was one big island with a marsh. The VI [6] stones were located, and the formula led him 500 feet to the now huge oak to which he attached a block and tackle on a limb overhanging well three. Although the mechanism was old it still worked, and the remaining gold and coin were brought up. He jammed the door at well 1 open.

He found the entrance to Hell was closed. He did not locate the trap door or the jewel box[es]. The box was destroyed. The poles mostly rotted were not replaced at the opening of each J (10?) foot level to CIII [103] feet. Everything was hastily filled. As there was a settlement on the mainland. After I [one] month and I [one] week his ship returned to take him and his LV [55] men with the treasure.

In MDCCXCV [1795] the Brittish navy found part of this document and ar[r]ived on the island to seaward locating well II [2] by the block and tackle and well I [1] that was jambed [jammed]. They were seen from the mainland and hastily left the island. XV [15] years later it was reported to Brother Roachfacould a man named McGinnis built a cabin over the trap and ▉▉▉▉▉▉▉▉▉▉▉▉ ▉▉▉▉▉▉. Continued excavations there have destroyed most of the workings of there. Subsequent settlement by a negro and the use of oxen to plow and move stone has resulted in further destruction of the project. Gas som[e]times still escapes into the swamp causing bubbles and groans with lightning lights over the water.

Locals say the place is haunted.

MCMLXV [1965] Tala Ko II

For those who have followed the history of the search for the legendary treasure on Oak Island they will not be disappointed unless they thought the treasure was still there to be found. The first thing that struck us was that the 1395 and 1769 dates matched the Roman numeral dates at the bottom of the Neck Map. It now seems we correctly interpreted those dates to be when the Oak Island treasures were deposited within the elaborate tunnel system beneath the island in 1395. The message also appears to confirm the legend about the young boy, coincidentally named Daniel McGinnis, who found the remains of a block and tackle found hanging from an oak tree above a depression in the ground on the island around the year 1795.

What so many believed about the legend was that the young McGinnis found what remained of the effort to hide the treasure, instead of what really happened. It appears what the boy actually found were the remains of the mechanics used to recover the treasure. For who would leave the equipment used to bury a treasure—a block and tackle attached to a rope hanging in

This page and next: The third message from Roberta was comprised of three pages of yet another box grid filled with another strange alphabet of symbols arranged in 19 columns and a total of 67 rows. The 8th symbol in the first row was a Hooked X used in the Roman numeral date of 1769. The message was dated to 1965, the most recent of all encrypted messages in the Cremona Document and signed "Tala Ko II." We suspect this is the son or grandson of Clyphus Lucinus Yzarbo who signed his name at the end of the Sacandaga Lake as "CLY" and "Tala Ko." (Courtesy of Donald Ruh)

a tree—and not backfill the hole to hide all evidence of hiding a valuable treasure? According to this message the recovery of the treasures was more complicated than originally thought. ███████████████

Diehard fans of the Oak Island mystery will no doubt recognize not only the name McGinnis, but "a negro", can only be referring to Samuel Ball, the African American slave who owned property on the island and reportedly became very rich in the 18th Century. That freed slave was named Samuel Ball.

The word "Hell" also jumped out at us and would appear in the two subsequent messages we decoded. We can only speculate they called one of the tunnels beneath Oak Island "Hell" because of the explosion of trapped gas that killed one of the men working in the tunnel using a lamp with a flame. This tragedy and the fire seen down below is likely where the name "Hell" came from used in the messages. What could have caused the fire naturally is hard to say for sure, but the most likely scenario is hydrogen sulfide gas seeping from decomposed plant material in the swamp area of the island. Hydrogen sulfide is heavier than oxygen—so it would sink into a tunnel, highly flammable, and is the most likely culprit to have killed the unfortunate man who was blown up working in one of the shafts, as well as the six men who died more modernly.

MESSAGE #4

The fourth message did not have anything to do with Oak Island.

MESSAGE #5

The fifth and final message took me two weeks to decipher and contained numerous errors, misspellings, and different spellings of the same words—such as an indigenous tribe in the area of Narragansett Bay spelled variously as: "Saconnet", "Saconet", and "Sakonet." The last message was also quite lengthy and dealt mainly with the underground tunnel system on Oak Island. The millions of people around the world who are fans of *The Curse of Oak Island* show will enjoy knowing exactly how the underground system was built and ultimately what happened there. The message incorporated the cipher phrase, first figured out by Janet, within the message a total of thirteen times. "The Power of God is within you," appears to have been incorporated and evenly spaced throughout the message to ensure the decoder was doing things correctly. If the phrase was incorrect, then it told you there was a mistake somewhere and to figure it out before continuing. Otherwise, the problems within the message only get worse. It is actually a brilliant way to ensure accuracy as the decoder does their work. I spent two weeks decoding the message even though I had a good grasp of the procedures. Without the regular occurrence of the cipher phrase, it would have been nearly impossible to decode the entire message accurately:

"(The Power of God is within you.) The Saconnet contract MCDLXXVI [1476] years the use of the observatory as gifted from

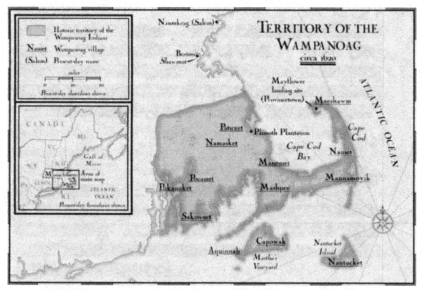

This map shows the various tribes within the Wampanoag nation at the beginning of the 17th Century. The Sakonnet tribe's territory included the eastern half of Narragansett Bay and Aquidneck Island where the Newport Tower stands to this day. (Internet)

the people to the Poor Knights of Christ. We leave the observatory construction for the northland as Nahookan [Native name for a constellation] *points south after Tachkanum* Native name for a constellation]. *XXXIV* [34] *days out with XXXIII* [33] *Saconet pledged to us the III* [3] *ships sail with the northland to Port Uhent t*[h]*e, sky darkens and a blou*[w] *comes S SE driven us N NW. Night is comming.*

Juan calls up a dowser. We need fresh water. ▮▮▮▮▮▮▮▮
▮▮▮▮▮▮▮▮▮▮▮▮▮▮▮▮▮▮▮▮▮▮▮▮▮▮▮▮▮▮▮▮▮▮▮
▮▮▮▮▮▮▮▮▮▮▮▮▮▮▮▮▮▮▮▮▮▮▮▮▮▮▮▮▮▮▮▮▮▮▮
▮▮▮▮▮▮▮▮▮▮▮▮▮▮▮▮▮▮▮▮▮▮▮▮▮▮▮▮▮▮▮▮▮▮▮
▮▮▮▮▮▮▮▮▮▮▮▮▮▮▮▮▮▮▮▮▮▮▮▮▮▮▮▮▮▮▮▮▮▮▮
▮▮▮▮▮▮▮▮▮▮▮▮▮▮▮▮▮▮▮▮▮▮▮▮▮▮▮▮▮ *Well*
I [1] finds I [1] natural cavity in soft rock I IV O [140] feet down a
Sakonet goes down with a lamp. There is a loud noise. Gas, he was
killed and is in pieces. Rogert Llebobone descends the next day by lot.
No more gas. ▮▮▮▮▮▮▮▮▮▮▮▮▮▮▮▮▮▮▮▮▮▮▮▮
▮▮▮▮▮▮▮▮▮▮▮▮▮▮▮▮▮▮▮▮▮▮▮▮▮▮▮▮▮▮▮▮▮▮▮
▮▮▮▮▮▮▮▮▮▮▮▮▮▮▮▮▮▮▮▮▮▮▮▮▮▮▮▮▮▮▮▮▮▮▮
▮▮▮▮▮▮▮▮▮▮▮▮▮▮▮▮▮▮▮▮▮▮▮▮▮▮▮▮▮▮▮▮▮▮▮

We have found an entrance to Hell. ▮▮▮▮▮▮▮▮
▮▮▮▮▮▮▮▮▮▮▮▮▮▮▮▮▮▮▮▮▮▮▮▮▮▮▮▮▮▮▮▮▮▮▮
▮▮▮▮ *Volcanic? Juan de Alvarez IV I [41] years. Lo Tutore VI VIII + I*
III [48 + 13] souls. Lionel De Walderne IV [4th] (44) years old. Le Vail-
lanet V VI [56] souls. Pierre D'armont III VII [37] years, Le Bonsaliere
VII IV [74] souls, Aristide De Porto III I [31] years, Da Roccae IX (9)
souls. ▮▮▮▮▮▮▮▮▮▮▮▮▮▮▮▮▮▮▮▮▮▮▮▮▮▮▮▮▮▮▮▮
▮▮▮▮▮▮▮▮▮▮▮▮▮▮▮▮▮▮▮▮▮▮▮▮▮▮▮▮▮▮▮▮▮▮▮
▮▮▮▮▮▮▮▮▮▮▮▮▮▮▮▮▮▮▮▮▮▮▮▮▮▮▮▮▮▮▮▮▮▮▮
▮▮▮▮▮▮▮▮▮▮▮▮▮▮▮▮▮▮▮▮▮▮▮▮▮▮▮▮▮▮▮▮▮▮▮
▮▮▮▮▮▮▮▮▮▮▮▮ *Every spar, mast, fitting nail, metal, and all wood*
rails, decking, siding to the waterline, (The power of God is within you)
with all canvas blocks, lines, rigging, and stores are removed ▮▮▮▮
▮▮▮▮ *A sea monster (whale?) is killed for its fat and oil* ▮▮▮▮▮▮
▮▮▮▮▮▮▮▮▮▮▮▮▮▮▮▮▮▮▮▮▮▮▮▮▮▮▮▮▮▮▮▮▮▮▮
▮▮▮▮▮▮▮▮▮▮▮▮▮▮▮▮▮▮▮▮▮▮▮▮▮▮▮▮▮▮▮▮▮▮▮
▮▮▮▮▮▮▮▮▮▮▮▮▮▮▮▮▮▮▮▮▮▮▮▮▮▮▮▮▮▮▮▮▮▮▮
▮▮▮▮▮▮▮▮▮▮▮▮▮▮▮▮▮▮▮▮▮▮▮▮▮▮▮▮▮▮▮▮▮▮▮

██*Alonzo*
rushes back. Voices by cavity. (The power of God is within you.) Ghosts.
Capt. Juan goes down with him. Well I [1] tunnel goes to cavity too.
Lionel and the Vaillent join Pierre. The III [3] captains talk. A plan is
made. With II III 0 [230] men work begins to secure a place for the relic
packed with wool within and without in an iron box. X [10] by IX [9]
by VI [6] inches high. Shelters are set up for the long courc[s]e. Captain
Philipe sails for Scotland come the frost. All else remain. Lionel sets VII
[7] Sakonnet south over land from the great river to the Temple of the
Goddess and the Vaillent returns as the snow flies. Philipe returns when
the seeds sprout with Aristide Deporto XXXIV [34] (y)ears old in the
Da Rocca with LIX [59] souls and Le bombe cinese de (The power of
God is within you.) MCCXCV [1295] and news of the betray[a]l and
capture of GM [Grand Master] Jaques DeMolay.

XXI [21] have died on the project. II [2] are hurt—CCCXI [311]
souls set work the heat from Hell makes work desired in the cold.
Workers draw lots. Lionel V [5ᵗʰ] XX [20] years old is pledged to a
Wampahog woman and he is told to put the silver cross on a little
island far south. He will not return to us but becomes the male head
at the Goddess Temple in Onteora. He is further pledged to go to █

██
██

██████████████████ *place the relic in a wood box with a carved rock atop*
it leave no trace (The power of God is within you.) above ground.

██
██
██
██
██
██

A wood box sealed with pitch w[a]s built III [3] feet long XIV
[14] inches wide I [1] foot high for the relic box and some gold bars
and coins. I [O]nce many know of the project Lionel, and I only know
the relic is not in its box, just a rock he is told to place a carved stone

(The power of God is within you.) over the relic as was cut in the Nabataean Temple at Petra that marked a treasure place.[30]

Using the bombe de Cinese

---

30 This appears to refer to the treasure Ralph De Sudeley recovered upon his return to Europe from North America.

is overlaid with gold. A cask bottom is fitted around the hole for a tight fit. Now th[e] system is to be tested. The Mickymacks bring us squash, beans, (The power of God is within you.) and maize ground. We kill I IV [14] bear and I VI [16] deer. We share with them. They show us how to make coats and clothes. It is MCCCXCV [1395]. Lionel VI [6th] grows strong like his father. He has II [2] sons and I [1] girl. I am his second son. Ueire [Uriel] pledged to the service of the angel Kay.

There is a lot to unpack in this message, but there are a few important takeaways that jump out. First, in the first sketch we received from Roberta that depicts Oak Island as two parts with the swamp in the middle, it also appears to show

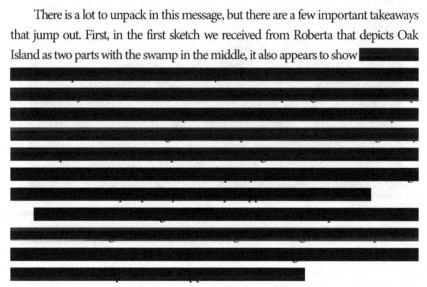

Construction of the underground works on Oak Island involved blasting away rock using gun powder first invented by the Chinese in the ninth century.[31] The third sketch uses the Theban alphabet—the secret alphabet often used

---

31 https://www.brown.edu/Departments/Joukowsky_Institute/courses/13things/7687.html#:~:text=Gunpowder%3A%20Origins%20in%20the%20East&text=%E2%80%9CGunpowder%2C%E2%80%9D%20as%20it%20came,for%20a%20life%2Dextending%20elixir

This page and next: The first and last pages of the fifth encrypted message was comprised of a total of eight pages and required a cipher phrase of twenty-four letters. Janet was the first to figure out the anagram was "The Power of God is Within You." The over 6,600 numbers within the grid system were divided into 24 parts. Only part of the message is transcribed here and involves only the information connected to the Oak Island mystery. (Courtesy of Donald Ruh)

by the Templars in the Cremona Document—to write in French and is titled, "The Chinese Bomb, 1295." Why the date of 1295 is used is unclear. However, it could refer to when the Templars acquired knowledge of gun powder, likely giving them an advantage in battle and construction. The sketch gives

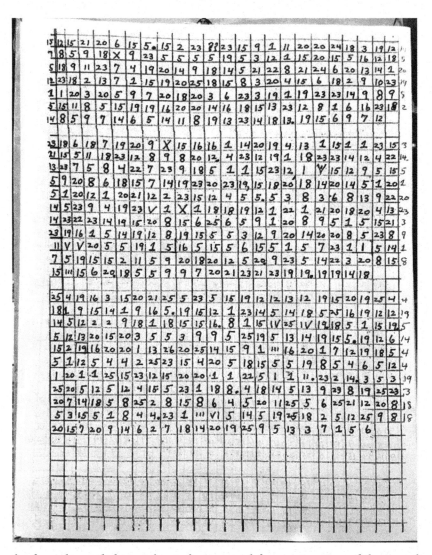

the formula needed to make explosives used for construction of the tunnel system. The French translated into English is as follows:

> *La toile [The web], De ce pouces XII [Of this inch 12], Mortier [Mortar], Le cavite arbre (The shaft cavity), Roc [rock], Pour melance de Bombe proportion [For bomb mix proportion], Pomme de terre pâtée XV [Mashed potatoes 15], Le soufre X [sulfur 10] and Nitre les cristal, Ecraser LXXV [Crush the crystals of Niter 75].*

The first page from Roberta shows detailed sketches of a cross-section of the tunnel system below Oak Island. The sketch also appears to show the water drainage system depicted on the new Oak Island map. The sketch is labeled in French, *Le Projet Souterrain* (The Underground Project) and shows where the "Relic Box" was hidden that contained what many believe was the "Holy Grail." (Courtesy of Donald Ruh)

COMMENTARY BY DON RUH: IUDEA'S DOCUMENTS

Scott has asked me to write my reasoning with regards to decrypting parts of the latest material we received from a woman referred to as Iudea. Bill described this name as a monogram of the Greek form of Christ's name.

The first two pages we received from this woman consisted of characters—symbols for numbers from zero to nine (Message #1). These are then

The second page from Roberta shows detailed sketches of mechanisms that operate floats and doors that allow groundwater to flow through tunnels and shafts that protect the treasures hidden below. (Courtesy of Donald Ruh)

combined to create sixteen more numbers totaling 26. Each standing for one letter of the alphabet A to Z. The plain text decrypted message is repeated below for the reader's convenience.

> *The power of God is within you. This is the final writing of this report. First done in MCCCVIII [1308] and revised three times till MCMVIII [1908]. The final putting of the relic is told here MDXCVII [1597]. In*

MCCCIV [1304] *Louis de Grimoard by order of Grand Master Jaques DeMolay ar[r]anged for three ships to embark from LaRochelle to locale de* [of] *Ramsey and Point de* [of] *Arye and Leith de* [of] *Saddel dans* [in] *le* [the] (Isle?) *de* [of] *Man with the pilot* (navigator?) *Francisco DeLeon, they embark to Harris West Isle for designer [architect?] Paolette Justinian Roach. Set sail Mars* [March] *XXI* [21] *for the brethren in northren* [Northern] *the northland. This is the account of the journey and the CCC* [300] *year project to secure the relic now held by Lionel de Waldern 111* [3rd] *XLIV* [44] *years old abo[a]rd le* [the] *Gaspard also captioned by Philip d' Armon with a crew of LVI* [56] *and I* [one] *chest of jewels and Jewelry with the relic. Philip d' Armont, relative of Pierre in Lo Tutore* [Italian: The Guardian] *with a crew of LXXIV* [74] *and III* [3] *chests of gold and silver bars. He also carries Ibrahim Muhammad Al-Zacara, maker of structure. Captain Juan de Alvarez from Garda Portugal in Le Vallant with chart maker Sotomon Yzarbo son of Licinius and a crew of*

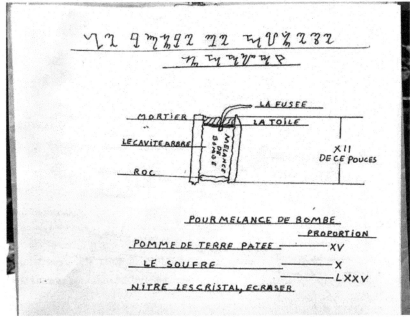

The third page from Roberta is a sketch titled using Theban characters to French, "The Chinese bomb, 1295." The page explains how to make such a bomb including the use of gun powder first invented by the Chinese in the 9th century. It appears the date of 1295 made with Theban characters represents when the Templars became aware of the Chinese invention of gun powder. (Courtesy of Donald Ruh)

LXVIII [68] *with V* [5] *chests of gold and silver coin completes the trio.
They ar*[r]*ive at the observatory in Juin* [June] *XXI* [21] *and leave Jillet*
[July] *XXI* [21] *for the land of the Wasuta and the Mickimacks.*

My first thought after reading this was that the first sentence has no
relevance to the remainder of the text. The Freemason's have secret hand-
shakes and body language to reflect distress etc., and I thought that this first
line may be something similar with regards to the Knights Templar. The
Templars also used word traps in their encoded material that the uninitiated
would be confounded in trying to decode a message. The reader should
think of walking down a wooded trail and stepping over a rotted log when,
snap, their foot is caught in a bear trap. Then with a woosh, a swinging log
with sharpened sticks hits them in the back. The traps can be avoided if one
knows where to look. These word traps often consist of missing letters that
when added to the message make subsequent words unreadable. The word
"the" written as "th" or "te" when having the missing letter added makes
the continuing message either readable or gibberish. Which method is often
indicated by an ambiguous symbol or mark somewhere on the original. A
little cross in the upper left corner of the message would be one such symbol.
Neither Scott nor I had the advantage of such information and trial and
error was the only process used, often an exasperating job.

The second part of the message consisted of 24 numbers in small boxes
across the page in blocks of twelve or so lines for 24 blocks of numbers. This
indicated to me that the missing key word or phrase would have 24 letters to it.
The key was, however, missing. This is when both Janet Wolter and I remem-
bered the first line of the previously decoded section and applied it to this
section with successful results. Scott decoded all of the message, a herculean
job, and sent the decoded message to me. In reading it I noticed several odd
letter K's. The material was accompanied by two pages of sketches. One apparently depicting underground digging and tunneling in a place we identified as
Oak Island. In reviewing Scott's translation, I noted that all of the odd letter K's
were associated with Roman numeral measurements. I also studied the two
pages of sketches apparently depicting the digging described in the text. When
I got to these lines something clicked mentally. "*The cavity is III* [3] *feet high
VI* [6] *feet in die*[a]*ameter. At KI* [1] *feet up is high water mark.*" Later on, I

again read, *"Within the structure is V [5] triangles I III [13] inches wide as V [5]nations work on the project. These are KI [1] inches apart.*

I looked at the portion of the sketch page matching the portion depicted below. This shows five triangular channels listed.

A being XIII (13) presumably inches apart wide XXI (21) apart. From the sketch I see the five triangles listed as XIII (13) thus agreeing with the text as I III (13) inches wide. Then I see in the sketch each triangular part is XXI (21) apart from each other thus the text must agree with the depiction. Therefore, the K = II (2) which is how it read on the original document, but Scott saw it as all of the other numbers relative to a letter and wrote K when it remains as II standing for "2" thus being 21 inches apart as stated in the text. Thus, applying this logic to all the other K's and in particular the previously mentioned *"At K [II] (2) I (1) feet up is high water mark.",* should read as *"At 21 feet up is high water mark."* In all subsequent instances where K is mentioned the number eleven as two is substituted, making a readable difference.

I would also call the reader's attention to the second numerical message when Scott shows it on page 83 the third line from the bottom there is an "XL" with a little extra bar, or "hook" or "tell" that would instruct the decoder of some "trap" in the text, perhaps the letter K.

CHAPTER 9:

THE SKULL, TREASURE, AND THE HOLY GRAIL

Now that the reader knows the truth about the extensive work done at Oak Island beginning in the fourteenth century and the stories behind the recovery of the treasures in 1769 and afterward, let's talk about the actual treasure recovered, and about the sacred relics that lived on the island for close to four centuries. As stated in the lengthy *The Power of God is Within You* message, the gold bars and coins spread out aboard all three ships, and the jewels and jewelry aboard the Le Gaspard were fantastic enough treasures, but the true and most sacred treasures brought over to North America had nothing to do with wealth. They were the relics people have speculated on for centuries and likely include the mysterious and sought after *Holy Grail*.

TALPIOT TOMB

Before anyone can make sense of the discussion to come about the skull and the cup of Christ, a little context is in order. In 1980 Jerusalem, a construction crew blasting the hillside in preparation for constructing the foundation of an apartment building in the East Talpiot neighborhood, they discovered a first century underground tomb. While not rare, this tomb had two rooms, an antechamber that was open to the southern sky and a small doorway cut into the relatively soft limestone bedrock leading to the burial chamber. Inside the burial chamber archaeologists discovered ten limestone boxes called *ossuaries*, inside small tunnels called *kukhims*. Seven of the ossuaries were inscribed with names, six in Aramaic and one in Greek. All seven names match individual members of the biblical family of Jesus. Shocking as this is to many people, it does appear this is the family tomb with some of the mortal remains of Jesus and other family members. For the curious, here are those names: "Jesus, son of Joseph", "James, son of Joseph, brother of Jesus", "Mariam called Mara (Written in Greek)", "Joses", "Judah son of Jesus", "Matthew", and "Maria."

This list of names is amazing, and the controversy it sparked when it first went public was huge, but there are other facts about the tomb that are just as shocking. When archaeologists excavated the tomb, they found three human skulls on the floor of the burial chamber in the east, south, and west quadrants. It is no coincidence this is where the three highest officers sit in a Masonic lodge or a Templar commandery. The skulls do not appear to be contemporaneous with when the ossuaries of the royal family were placed in the tomb, nearly two millennia ago. Instead, it appears someone entered the tomb sometime in the intervening history and placed them. The most likely candidates are the Knights Templar in the early twelfth century, after they captured the holy city of Jerusalem. Keep in mind, the leadership of the Templars, including the first Grand Master Hugh de Payans, were bloodline descendants of Jesus and his family. This is why the Poor Knights of Christ knew where the tomb was—it was their family tomb as well.

This first-century tomb was discovered 1980 when a construction crew blasted a hillside in preparation for building an apartment building in the East Talpiot neighborhood of Jerusalem. The antechamber was destroyed but the entrance to the burial chamber remained intact. (Internet)

The reason they went in is obvious, to recover the remains of their ancestors, as the Roman Catholic Church had elevated them to literal God-like status. The family knew the truth and recovered the remains before the Church found them and spread the relics all across Christendom used to extract more wealth from the flock and spread more lies. The Templars removed the bones of their ancestors for safe keeping. The three skulls on the floor of the burial chamber were likely three Templar knights killed during the siege of Jerusalem who have been honored to have been symbolic guardians of their ancestral tomb. The number three, so sacred within Templarism and Freemasonry, is a huge clue to who was responsible.

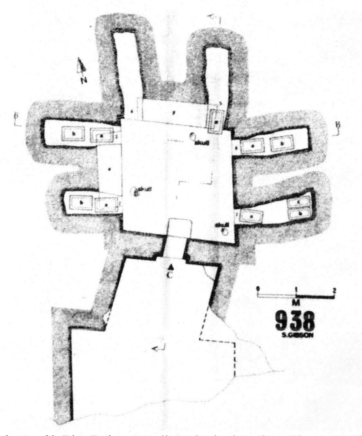

This plan view of the Talpiot Tomb was mapped by Israeli archaeologist, Shimon Gibson, in 1980. The antechamber at the bottom of this drawing was mostly destroyed, but the burial chamber remained intact. Inside were two shelves and six niches that contained a total of ten ossuaries. (Tabor and Jacobovici, Page 29, 2012)

THE RELIC

From the very beginning in 2008, from the first encrypted message left by Bill Jackson, it was clear to us the original Templar knights led by Grand Master Hugh De Payans, had recovered the remains of a man inside an ossuary from in an ancient ritual chamber deep underneath the South Wall in the early twelfth century. Quoting the narrative, *"This man died when his head was cut off with a very sharp axe."*, and *"There is a name and I read a little Ivri [Hebrew] it is to me that falls the making out of what is written. It is Yon. Bernrd bags the bones."*

That man had to be from the first century since the Essenic ossuary culture in Jerusalem only lasted roughly a century, ending in 70 AD when the Romans defeated the Jews and the tradition ended. We deduced that man had to be John the Baptist and the Templar's had his remains which included his skull.

In these latest messages from Roberta, there are multiple mentions of the "skull", and the "relic." We believe both terms refer to the same skull which Templars recovered under the South Wall. There are multiple facts that support this, most notably the importance of John the Baptist to Freemasonry—he's one of the patron saints of the guild.[32] Masonic lodges are dedicated to the Holy Saints: John the Apostle, John the Evangelist, and John the Baptist—but prior to circa 1600, their lodges were dedicated only to the Baptist. His feast day is June 24th and is celebrated with dinners and other events throughout the world within Freemasonry.

The medieval Knights Templar were much more secretive about their veneration for the Baptist, the biological ancestor of several members of the leadership of the order. In fact, when the order was suppressed on October 13, 1307, one of the charges leveled against those who were arrested and put on trial by the Roman Catholic Church was worshiping the bearded head called Baohomet[33]. Indeed, it appears the charge might have been true as the head of the Baphomet was, in all likelihood, the head of John the Baptist, recovered under the South Wall almost two centuries earlier. The skull and bones flag the fugitive Templar pirates flew to intimidate their enemies no doubt represented their patron saint of John the Baptist. Besides the latest messages from Roberta putting an end to the mystery of the skull of John the Baptist, the Sinclair/Wemyss journals also make mention of the obviously

---

32 https://californiafreemason.org/2022/12/20/patron-saint/
33   https://www.britannica.com/topic/Baphomet

sacred item they called the "Bahumet" (Baphomet?). In entries made by James Wemyss (1560–1640) on September 22, 1627, and July 22, 1628, he made mention of a sacred object that took precedent even over gold:

> 22 September 1627
> The Behumet (?) and remaining gold from Laon has been placed in the Cave of Thieves where we can protect and care for it. There it will remain until the proper time when we can begin our voyage to the Western Lands."

> 22 July 1628
> Word has finally arrived from our brethren who have traveled to the Western Lands. They have found a spot of perfection for the Behumet and the treasure but say that Nova Scotia (Acadia) is now overrun with French and the English.

Twelve years later James Weems' grandson, David Wemyss (1610–1679), mentions the Behumet on April 20, 1640:

> My father has passed to me the journals of our forefathers and the obligation to complete the Covenant of the Brethren who guard the Templar Treasure and the Behumet. I pray that I am worthy and begin to read the journals.

On April 25, 1665, David's son, James Wemyss (1633–1714) again mentions the Behumet:

> The weather is fine, and the ships have been provisioned. Crew with sailing and mining experience have been assembled and we leave tomorrow for the western coast of Scotland to remove the artifacts and gold still resident at the Abbey. We have already secured the Behumet and gold from the Cave of Thieves on board the lead ship the Balfour to be protected by the 12 Brethren aboard. Once we leave the shores of Scotland, we will visit Greenland for fresh water and hope to reach Nova Scotia by the 1st of June."

From the Cremona Document:

> "In 1769 (MDCCLXIX) Capt'n Timothy MaClarin landed on the seaward side of the small island. He saw it was one big island with a marsh.

The 6 (VI) stones were located, and the formula led him 500 feet to the now huge oak to which he attached a block and tackle on a limb overhanging well three. Although the mechanism was old it still worked, and the remaining gold and coin were brought up. He jammed the door at well 1 open.

He found the entrance to Hell was closed. He did not locate the trap door or the jewel box(es). The box was destroyed. The poles mostly rotted were not replaced at the opening of each J (10?) foot level to CIII (103) feet. Everything was hastily filled. As there was a settlement on the mainland. After I (one) month and I (one) week his ship returned to take him and his LV (55) men with the treasure.

In MDCCXCV (1795) the Brittish navy found part of this document and ar(r)ived on the island to seaward locating well II (2) by the block and tackle and well I (1) that was jambed (jammed). They were seen from the mainland and hastily left the island. XV (15) years later it was reported to Brother Roachfacould a man named McGinnis built a cabin over the trap ████████████████████ ████████████ Continued excavations there have destroyed most of the workings of there. Subsequent settlement by a negro and the use of oxen to plow and move stone has resulted in further destruction of the

This relic box contains a human skull used in Knights Templar rituals and is symbolically connected to the head of John the Baptist. (Wolter, 2023)

project. Gas som(e)times still escapes into the swamp causing bubbles and groans with lightning lights over the water.

Locals say the place is haunted. The relics are assumed safe. ▆▆▆▆ ▆▆▆▆ *remains. The skull below Victoria was retrieved.*

MCMLXV (1965) Tala Ko II"

THE HOLY GRAIL

The cache of documents received from Roberta was the greatest gift to the Cremona Document story and finally put the mystery of the treasure of Oak Island to rest once and for all. What hasn't been put to bed in the pantheon of Knights Templar mysteries is the answers to the questions surrounding the Holy Grail. What is it and where is it now? Speculation about the grail has led to many theories as to what it might be. Some say it is the cup used by Jesus at the last supper; others believe it is ancient knowledges of alchemy, navigation, and astronomy; while others believe it is the womb of sacred feminine that carries forward the bloodline of Jesus himself. Still others believe it is the achievement of spiritual enlightenment that some say is the true path to heaven. Or maybe it was the establishment of the long sought after Free Templar State—the New Atlantis as told by Francis Bacon, the New Jerusalem, the sanctuary to the west where people could live free from the tyranny of the monarchs of Europe and the persecutions of the Roman Catholic Church—what we now call the United States of America. These are all worthy candidates for the title of the Grail, but there is one more possibility that the documents suggest.

One doesn't need to be a scholar to realize the importance of the skull of John that Baptist to the Knights Templar and the ideological traditions that took their place. Freemasonry is one such tradition that clearly weaved its way through the medieval military order. All of their lodges are dedicated to the Baptist who was the one who initiated Jesus all those years ago. The Baptist was more important than Jesus—who was lionized by the Church over the centuries—while John was pushed into the shadows. It is now clear with the latest material, the all-important and sacred relic was the skull of John the Baptist, who is now being "resurrected" to his rightful place within the tradition. His skull has completed the same journey as the Knights Templar beginning in

Jerusalem in the early twelfth century and finding its way to North America and finally to the United States after the country was founded.

Maybe that skull of John is the real Holy Grail? Like the story of Jesus and the crucifixion, John was beheaded and killed, and then it took 1,800 years for his skull to make it to the sanctuary after the founding of the United States, in an allegorical resurrection of his spirit embodied by the brotherhood that completed the Covenant, we now call Freemasonry. It's as good a candidate for the Holy Grail as anything else, and who knows, maybe there are other sacred skulls brought west by the Templars. Besides John, could Jesus and Mary Magdalene be here as well?

Chapter 10:

Veracity of the Documents and Conclusions

The burning question for Don and I, and for those of you reading this book, has always been, is this fantastic story about Oak Island really true? For that matter, is the history presented within these documents surrounding the Templars extended activities—that ultimately led to the founding of the United States—true as well? There are many reasons why Don and I not only believe this history is true, but we *know* it's true. The chapter that follows are the reasons we know these documents are authentic and demand a major rewrite of the history of the Knights Templar, the story of Oak Island, the founding of America, and possibly the answer to the enduring mystery of the Holy Grail. Let's start with the tangible evidence that is irrefutable and serves as the firm foundation to prove the veracity of the documents.

The Shipwreck in Newfoundland

Perhaps the most compelling argument that the Cremona Document is an authentic compendium of documents and maps is the remains found of one of six ships in the flotilla led by Sir Ralph De Sudeley that was scuttled off the southern coast of Newfoundland in 1178. In August of 1971, after securing a few pages of the document from the seller, Bill Jackson asked Don Ruh to accompany him to Newfoundland to scuba dive to look for the ship. Don and Bill, along with two locals, found the remains of the ship in roughly 35 feet of water.[34]

---

34 The details of this discover can be found in our forthcoming book: *The Templar Covenant in America: The Truth About the Hooked X*™

In 2022, Don found a notebook—that originally belonged to his father—which he took with him on the trip to Newfoundland with Bill. The notes are very detailed and include sketches of the parts of the ship they were able to bring up onto their vessel. I chided Don for not producing the vitally important notebook earlier and he shot back saying, "I forgot all about it."

It's a good thing Don finally found the book for it provides vital corroborating evidence to Bill Jackson's twelve-page written narrative about the discovery of the ship which convinced him the information in the Cremona Document material was indeed true. This prompted Bill to go back to Italy and buy the rest of the document from Mr. Benvenuto.

On the second day of diving they pulled up the base portion of the mast that still had parts of the deck of the ship attached with wooden pegs. The next day they found three sections of the keel from the same area as the mast. Attached to the mast was a brass strap with a stone used to tighten

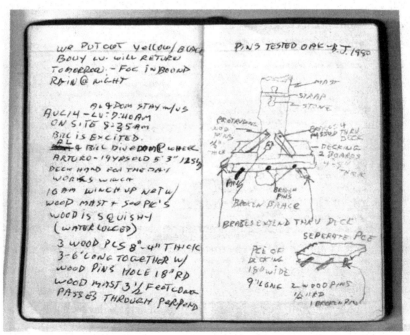

On August 14, 1971, after having marked the location of the object on the bottom with a buoy the previous day, an excited Bill Jackson and Al discover and pull into the boat using a winch, part of the wooden mast and decking of a wooden ship. Don described how the waterlogged "squishy" floorboards contain wooden pegs instead of metal nails and he included a detailed sketch of the mast still attached to the floorboards. The mast was comprised of two pieces that were joined together by a brass strap tightened by a wedge-shaped stone. (Courtesy of Donald Ruh)

the strap that had carvings on each end. Bill took the stone home with him while the remains of the ship they recovered were given to local authorities. The carvings were important symbols to the Templars and their ancestors who also sailed the seas centuries and millennia before them. The first was a carving of a Tanit symbol, the ancient Goddess of the Phoenicians—who were master mariners dating back thousands years to at least 1500-300 BC. Tanit—whose origins go back to the constellation of Virgo, the Goddess constellation in the heavens—provided protection to mariners who sailed the dangerous seas of antiquity. The second carving was an octopus-looking creature that had five legs instead of eight. Bill Jackson wrote he believed the carving was the wilted five-petaled rose of the House of Migdal. In either case, it likely was another symbol of protection to the brave people of the ancient seas. The stone found on the scuttled ship with the carvings was photographed by Bill and is seen in two pieces after apparently being broken.

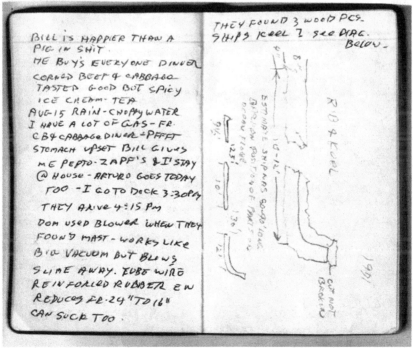

Bill Jackson apparently knew what they had found, yet kept the information to himself. On August 15, 1971, they again dove on the wreck and pulled up three, approximately ten-foot-long sections of the keel of the estimated eighty to ninety-foot-long ship. (Courtesy of Donald Ruh)

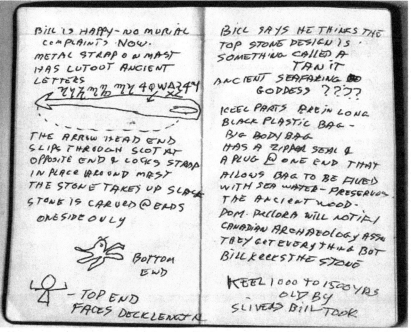

Pages 14 and 15 include a description and sketches of the brass strap, which contained sixteen symbols etched onto the surface, and the wedge-shaped stone which had two carvings. The bottom end has a now-familiar image of a five-legged octopus and on the top end was what looked like an ancient goddess symbol called a Tanit. In what looks like a later entry, Don wrote, "Keel 1000 to 1500 y[ea]rs old by sliver Bill took." (Courtesy of Donald Ruh)

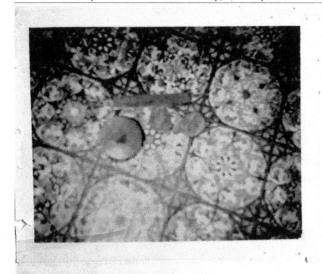

This picture, taken in 1975, shows the brass seal found inside the ornament on the Hudson River, the brass bar found on Prince Edward Island, and the wedged stone (broken in half) found on the mast of the De Sudeley ship in Newfoundland in 1971. (Courtesy of Donald Ruh)

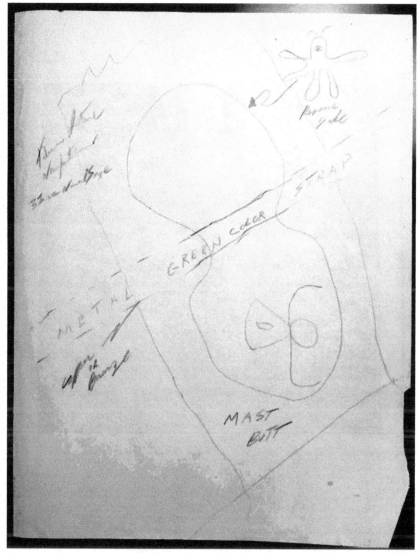

This sketch was drawn in red pencil by Bill Jackson of the brass strap and wedged stone attached to the mast of Ralph de Sudeley's scuttled ship of in the late twelfth century. The notes were made shortly after he and Donald Ruh discovered the ship while scuba diving in Newfoundland in August of 1971 and say "Theban stone Newfoundland, 32 inches not to size", "Reverse side", and "Copper or bronze". (Courtesy of Donald Ruh)

The discovery of the sunken twelfth-century Templar ship by Bill and Don is remarkable and provides powerful evidence supporting the veracity of the Cremona Document material. This discovery alone is extremely compelling but is only the beginning.

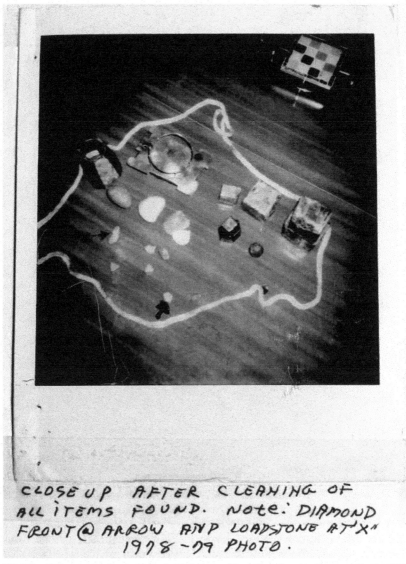

CLOSE UP AFTER CLEANING OF
ALL ITEMS FOUND. NOTE: DIAMOND
FRONT @ ARROW AND LOADSTONE AT "X"
1978 - 79 PHOTO.

This Polaroid photo is one of several taken by Bill Jackson of the artifacts found in Altomara's Cave in 1977. The silver necklace found inside the largest metal container to the far right encircles the artifacts. The ink arrow points to a 10-carat rough diamond. (Courtesy of Donald Ruh)

ALTOMARA'S TOMB

After finding De Sudeley's scuttled ship, Bill was highly motivated and returned to Rome to purchase the entire document from Gustave Benvenuto. He then translated the entire encrypted message and learned about the female navigator of the expedition, Altomara. She guided a party of twenty-six who were dropped off at the mouth of the St. Lawrence River, who then hiked to the Temple of the Goddess on Hunter Mountain in the Catskills of what is now known as New York state. During their almost two-year stay, Altomara was killed by a warring tribe. Her body was burned, and the remains were placed inside an urn which was then interred into a small cave on the mountain near the temple, along with many offerings. The cave was and then sealed with a large boulder. Bill and Don spent six years together, from 1971-1977, hiking the Catskills searching for the Temple of the Goddess and Altomara's tomb as told in De Sudeley's deposition taken upon his return to Europe in Seborga, Italy, in 1180.

On October 11, 1977, Bill discovered the tomb along with two other colleagues. Several months later after failing to move the boulder, they blasted it to enter the cave and recover the urn with Altomara's remains. This further cemented the veracity of the document for Bill and prompted him to write a book about it. Sadly, the book was never completed due in part to his frustration with academia which included a disappointing encounter with Harvard scholar, Dr. Barry Fell.

THE SINCLAIR/WEMYSS JOURNALS

Perhaps the most compelling and powerful evidence supporting the veracity of the Cremona Document are the numerous instances of the same events also appearing in the Sinclair/Wemyss journals.

Antonio Zeno: In book two of Earl Henry Sinclair's journals, beginning with an entry on May 31, 1390, he writes about the famous Italian navigator, Antonio Zeno, recounting details that parallel specific information from the *Zeno Narrative*, a document about the explorers' activities in the North Atlantic and rumored landing in North America published by a direct descendant in 1558. Masonic scholar Robert Cooper published a book in 2004 that included both an Italian and English version of the narrative that includes thirteen specific details that directly match information written by Earl Henry Sinclair. One item specifically is worth noting above the rest, since it was wrong in the original narrative, but accurate in the Sinclair journal. The narrative mentions a letter written by Nicolo Zeno to his brother Antonio. However, in the journals it is abundantly clear that Nicolo is not a brother, he is in fact, Antonio's _father_. On July 3, 1394, Earl Henry wrote:

> _Captain Nicolo has written to his brother Carlos Zeno in Venice about a voyage of discovery he wishes to make. His ship being destroyed he requests that Carlos send Antonio, the son of Nicolo, to Orkney with another ship. He should arrive in the spring. Captain Nicolo has now left for Groenland [Greenland] to explore the western coastline and will return in 2 months._

It is worth mentioning there is a Roman numeral date of 1395 on the lambskin map presumed to have been drawn by Antonio Zeno who was also a cartographer. Below the 1395 date is a curious siglum of the navigator that includes some interesting esoteric symbols. There appears to be a deliberately made "M" within the artistically made "Z" initial, as well as a "fish" symbol at the base of the far-right leg of the "M." Fish symbols are also seen in the one picture we have of Earl Henry's entries as well as in a picture of the crew list of the "Somnium." Scott wrote in detail about these symbols in his Cryptic Code of the Templars in America book that are still used to this day by initiates in certain Templar traditions.[35]

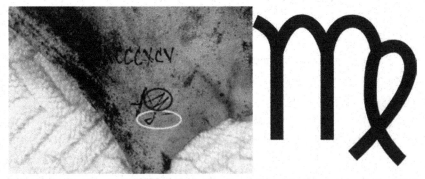

On the lambskin map purportedly made by the explorer Antonio Zeno, is the Roman numeral date of 1395 and his siglum. The siglum appears to incorporate two esoteric symbols used by the Knights Templar: the "M" and the "fish" symbol (Left). These two symbols combined also make the astrological symbol for Virgo (right), the sixth symbol of the zodiac. (Wolter, 2016/Internet)

35 Wolter, Pages 86-88 and Pages 101-110, 2019.

Could there also be a veiled reference to the Goddess—and the constellation of Virgo—in the Latin "M" on line eight of the Kensington Rune Stone? In 2002, while generating a microscopic photo-library of the Kensington inscription, I documented an intentionally made punch mark at the bottom of the far-right leg of the Latin "M". At the time, it was unknown why the carver made the mark that had been previously unnoticed. It appears the answer is that the obviously initiated Cistercian monk was quietly invoking the Goddess to protect the precious Templar land claim.

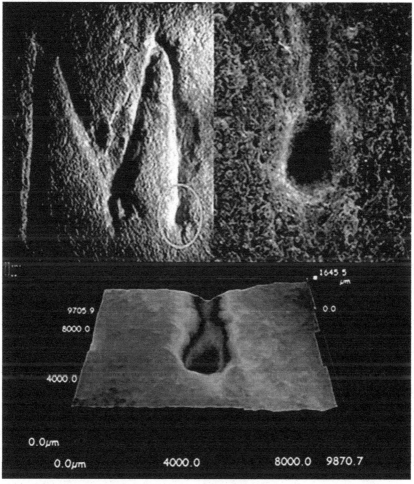

The carver of the Kensington Rune Stone added a deep punch mark on the lower end of the right leg of the "M" in an apparent acknowledgment to the Goddess—most likely in this case—Mary Magdalene, and to protect the Knights Templar land claim. (2002/2011, 2011)

The name of what must be the same Antonio Zeno mentioned in the Sinclair/Wemyss Journals appears twice on Map 8 of the Cremona Document material. On the back side of Map 8 there are two separate paragraphs, one written in French the other in Latin. The French paragraph was written by the cartographer who, in 1858, compiled the voluminous number of Templar maps drawn over the centuries. The narrative contains vital historical information—including names and dates—and closes with thought-provoking prose that only a person in his position could have written. Within his summary of the work of previous cartographers he wrote, "...the maps of Antonio Zeno 1398..."

To the right of the long paragraph is a much shorter paragraph written in French that translated into English reads: *"From the map of Zeno comes this declaration, we make the deposit on a-min by his grace and that of O-Gaia."* In light of the information presented in the Sinclair/Wemyss Journals, this "deposit" appears to have been singled out and of some significance beyond the other treasures described in the entries that were deposited in the fourteenth century. It is clear Antonio Zeno played an important role in the early chapters of the Templars in America, and a big role in the vetting of both documents.

Dog Island

Some of the most compelling entries in the journals were written by Earl Henry after his fleet of ships were besieged by storms off the coast of Nova Scotia, costing the lives of many men and ships both in 1395 and 1398. One particularly interesting passage made by Earl Henry on August 1, 1398, brings in the name of an island we could find no reference to anywhere on the Internet:

> *We have labored for many weeks to free the Katherine and are unable to do so while her cargo is onboard. We have felled trees to the west and have attempted to dig a ditch filled with water that she might slide into the harbor on the other side of the island which we have named "Dog Island". The island is uninhabited and has no evidence of having been visited by the native people recently. At this time five other ships have been located and lodge in the harbor which we have named for* ▇▇▇▇▇▇▇▇▇▇▇▇ *In our search for*

the other ships, we have located the wreck of the Ortus ▇▇▇▇▇▇
▇▇▇▇ *and are still searching for survivors, two of my own kinsmen
amongst them.*

We have identified "Dog Island" as McNab Island near Halifax, Nova
Scotia, but nowhere can we find it ever being called that in the past. It took
six years before we found a reference on Map 8 which contains a total of
thirteen maps. Map 12 (Deuze) is labeled in French, *Le isle de Chien* (The
Island of Dog). This discovery was shocking to say the least and provided a
huge, independent boost of credibility to the Sinclair/Wemyss Journals.

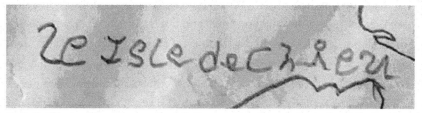

On the Twelfth part of Map 8 that came from the Spartan Box is a distorted version of McNabb Island that is
labeled in French, "Le isle de Chien" (The Island of Dog). The only other known reference to McNabb Island ever
being called Dog Island is in the Sinclair/Wemyss journals in the late 14th Century. (Courtesy of Donald Ruh)

NEWPORT TOWER[36]

What is arguably the crown jewel of evidence of the ideological descendants of the medieval Templars in North America shouldn't come as a
surprise if it is found in both sets of documents. The Newport Tower isn't
mentioned in the Sinclair/Wemyss Journals until a then 28-year-old John
Weems Jr. wrote the following on June 25, 1769:

> *Brother Peleg has shown us what is called the Newport Tower. It
> has been here longer than the village was founded. Some say it is a grain
> mill while others say it was built by the Templars to mark the seasons
> and to claim the surrounding area for settlement. It is the most unusual
> place I have ever seen, and I am fascinated by the methods in which
> it was constructed. As an engineer I can see how it must have been
> difficult to construct the tower using pressure points. It has 2 stories
> and has recesses in the stone for a fire and small windows that look out*

---

36   See page X for a photo of the Newport Tower.

to all the directions of the compass. The sun enters through a different window each season and whoever built the tower had a great knowledge of astronomy. The watcher Baraqijal would have been proud.

The quarry stone used is also unusual and must have taken a great amount of effort to bring to this site. I have sketched a picture of the tower for my wife as I'm certain she would love to see it. After staying the night, we will be returning to Philadelphia. I am anxious to talk to my father about what I have seen. I wonder if his recollections are the same as mine.

The Cremona Document has even more dramatic information about the tower that sheds new light on when and how it was constructed to incorporate all the well-documented astronomical alignments that still amaze six centuries after its initial construction. On the Narragansett Map that Bill Jackson took pictures of, there is a dot along a line of latitude on Aquidneck Island at the exact location of the Newport Tower. If there was any doubt

On part nine (Neuf) of Map 8, which was copied from animal skin onto paper in 2010, a dot on Aquidneck Island marks the location of the Newport Tower. This map was apparently first drawn in 1368 and is marked with a line that reads in French, "Place of the observatory." (Courtesy of Donald Ruh)

about this dot representing the tower, Map 8 removes it. The ninth (Neuf) map is a replication of the Narragansett Map with one distinct difference. There is a line running from the same dot terminating at these words in French, *Place de L'observetoire* (Place of the observatory).

This isn't all the document has to say about the important stone and mortar structure. On the second of the two pages of notes, written in French, Don received from his friend Bill Jackson via the estate of John Drake in 2019. Notation number 22 conveys some amazing information:

> *The observatory is built here. The hut of the day observers is on the right and the night observers on the left. The field of measurement surrounded by a stone wall separated them from numerous slabs and wooden poles. Henri remains here to oversee the construction.*

This comment was originally written by a scribe who must have been present during the initial phases of construction in the fourteenth century. It confirms what many researchers already knew—the Newport Tower is first and foremost an astronomical observatory. The "day and night observers" indicate the structure was to incorporate both solar and lunar alignments, as has been demonstrated by people like the late William Penhallow—Professor of Astronomy at the University of Rhode Island. The description that says *"...a stone wall separated them* [observers] *from numerous slabs and wooden poles..."* is reminiscent of the ancient standing stone sites across the world marking the solstices, equinoxes, phases of the moon, the movements of the planets, constellations, and precession of the equinoxes. Even the key question asked of when this mysterious stone and mortar structure was built is addressed.

The invisible map on the back of the back containing this entry has a Roman numeral date of 1368 (MCCCLXVIII). One could also argue the timing of construction of the tower is confirmed with the name "Henri" within the passage. Is it the Scottish Earl who visited the Western Lands three times during his lifetime according to his journals? Let's take a closer look at some of the entries and see what light might be shed.

While visiting the Norwegian King in 1368, Earl Henry wrote an interesting passage that instantly brought to mind a possible connection to the Kensington Rune Stone inscription on June 1, 1368:

> *This day while we supped with the King's court, we listened to a seaman who has returned from the Western Lands and tells us of the abundance of land and game past the ice banks of Groenland [Greenland]. It makes me anxious to travel to the Western Banks again as I did when I was a child. He tells of the journey and how he was forced to stay for many years before he was allowed to return. He makes me wonder of the 30 men who had left Norway in the Spring of 1358. I pray that they are well, and they will return soon.*

Upon his return to Scotland nearly two months later, Henry wrote about a party of Norse Templars on July 26, 1368:

> *I have spoken with the brethren regarding my concerns for the men who had traveled to the Western Banks in the spring of 1358. No word has been received from them, but Brother Cameron has said that none is expected. They were instructed to find suitable land for settlement and that more would follow. He acknowledged that they were men of the Craft and included monks with herbal knowledge. Because of the political unrest in Scotland no additional Brethren have been sent. It might be several years before another journey can be planned.*

The mention of "30 men" who left Norway in 1358 instantly recalled the Kensington party. The inscription is written in Old Swedish, a time when Sweden was under the rule of Norway. Henry also mentions he was told the party was "…to find suitable land for settlement…" This implies they were not coming back, which is consistent with the argument I have made in my previous books about the Kensington Rune Stone being a Templar land-claim. This passage provides strong support to that argument. These entries make clear there was a broader network of the ideological descendants of the Knights Templar whose long-range plan was to establish a new home in North America. This plan comes into full view in an entry Henry wrote twenty-seven years later on May 1, 1395:

> *Our goal is to find a better route to the empires of China further south than the ice-covered lakes and suitable land for settlement beyond the boundaries of Groenland which we visit on our journey.*

We also travel with 120 remaining Knights Templars, descendants of those at Bannockburn under my grandfather's rule in search of a free Templar state. We search for suitable places to transfer the Templar treasure hidden in Scotland.

Circling back to the Newport Tower, timing-wise the party that left Norway in 1358 are in all likelihood, the same party who not only carved the Kensington Rune Stone land claim in 1362 but were also involved in the laying out of the alignments prior to construction of the Newport Tower in 1368. I will remind the reader of the indisputable connection between the two sites I wrote about in my 2009 book, *The Hooked X™: Key to the Secret History of North America*—the long-range alignment between the Kensington Stone site and the Newport Tower, through the only two keystones in the west/northwest archway of the structure. While the entries do not make it clear if the "Henri" in the 22nd Note is the same Earl Henry Sinclair who wrote the journals, what is clear is the documents present strong and possibly conclusive evidence the Newport Tower was not built as a colonial windmill and is, in fact, a late medieval astronomical observatory constructed by the ideological descendants of the Knights Templar. The entries in Earl Henry's journals, and the material in the Cremona Document provide exciting new details on these long pondered historical enigmas.

As if giving an emphatic stamp of approval, both pages and the "invisible" Theban text on the back of page two of the notes have the Hooked X symbol incorporated into the text as if giving a final stamp of authenticity to the documents and the information contained within them.

Father Richards

What might be the most amazing entry in the journals was written by a then-twelve-year-old Henry Sinclair. It wasn't until reading the entries a second time that the significance became apparent to me. He wouldn't learn till later in his life about what we call the Kensington party, having left Norway for the Western Lands in 1358. Armed with this knowledge, reading the entries the second time through led to a starling realization in what Henry wrote on November 22, 1357:

I spent the day at the forge with my father learning about the feast of Weyland the Norse God of the Smiths. I am clumsy at the forge but respect those who are very clever. The smiths are creating nails and rivets for a boat to travel to the west banks in the spring. Father Dominic says that Father Richardus will accompany them with the seven new acolytes.

The only boat mentioned that needed nails and rivets for traveling to the Western Lands in the spring of 1358 was the Kensington party that left from Norway. This discovery is interesting enough, but the real bombshell was in the last sentence. The reader might recall the first line of the Kensington inscription reads, "*8 Goths* [Gotlanders] *and 22 Northmen* [Norwegians]..." If the journals are a reliable indicator, the eight Goths might be the, "... men of the Craft including monks with herbal knowledge..." mentioned in Henry's July 26, 1368, entry. According to my research into the esoteric and symbolic aspects of the Kensington inscription, it appears the *"seven new acolytes"* and Father Richardus are being acknowledged and intentionally singled out using what many scholars have called "strange runes."

In 2019, I published what I called the "Confirmation Code" within the Kensington inscription. The code involves the number of "strange, never before seen" runic symbols used throughout the twelve lines of the inscription to confirm the importance of four sacred numbers. These include the 8 g/u runes, 10 w/v runes, 14 individual numbers and the 22 Hooked X symbols used for the letter "a". If we look carefully at the 8 g/u runes we see there are actually 7 backwards "g" runes, and one unique "u" rune that resembles the "g" but has a little more going on. There is an extra horizontal bar on the bottom of the vertical stave and two punch marks in the open upper half instead of one. Could these special seven "g" runes be symbolic of the "seven new acolytes" and the even more unique "u" be emblematic of Father Richardus? If so, then it could mean the Master of the eight Goths/monks, Father Richardus, was the carver of the Kensington Rune Stone inscription.

The incredible discovery of Father Richardus was made in July of 2016 when the Sinclair/Wemyss Journals were first brought to my attention. It wasn't until March of 2021, when the Spartan Box was opened when the name Father Richards appeared again. On the back of Map 8 there is a long narrative

The Kensington Rune Stone has seven "g" runes with a single punch in the upper half, and one "u" rune with one short horizontal line on the lower part of the vertical stave and two punch marks in the upper half. Both are unusual Scandinavian runes. Could these eight runes allegorically represent the "seven acolytes" and Father Richards by symbolizing the new initiates and their Master? (Wolter, 2002)

written by the mysterious "CLY", whom reveals himself to be Clyphus Lucinus Yzerbo. He wrote about the map makers and Templar ship captains he and others before him sailed with, beginning in the twelfth century through his compilation of all the work now known as Map 8 in 1908. Roughly a third of the way through his narrative he wrote something shocking that could not have been made up or dismissed in any way as a coincidence, "...the acolyte of Father Richards..." Having Father Richards appear in both documents is a powerful, if not conclusive, testament to their authenticity.

Sacred Numbers

Another very rare aspect of information found in both sets of documents is the use of sacred numbers. Only those who have been initiated into Freemasonry and Templarism have any knowledge of the sacred numbers 8, 13, and 21, and were a telltale calling card to their brethren, saying, "this is us." These three numbers are part of the Fibonacci Sequence that relates to the sacred, and secret, veneration of the life-giving Goddess. The Sinclair/ Wemyss Journals begin with a powerful clue to understanding the ideology of the Scottish clans in the fourteenth century with the first entry written by the young Henry Sinclair on his eighth birthday, November 5, 1353:

> *My father gave me this journal for the celebration of my 8th birthday. He tells me to write about things I want to remember when I am a man. This year Father Dominic will teach me Latin, French, Gaelic and Norwegian. Father has promised to take me fishing with him in the spring. I can't wait to see the western banks and want to catch lots of fish."*

Later entries continue to display a deep understanding and reverence of these sacred numbers, more especially when it came to the crew lists of the ships. There was a total of 8 ships on both the 1395 and 1398 voyages that made their way to the western lands.

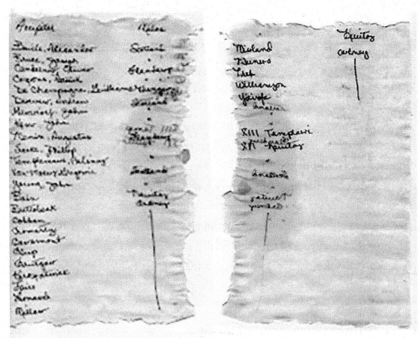

The first and last names of the thirteen Templar knights appear at the top of a list of names of crewmen aboard the Accipiter. It was one of eight ships that sailed to the Western Lands led by Earl Henry Sinclair in 1395. (Wolter, 2016)

In the crew lists for the 8 ships on the 1395 Sinclair expedition there were 13 Templar Knights aboard the Accipiter, Itienere, Repostus and the Speculator. There were 21 knights aboard the Perequin and the Ortus.

Here are a couple more examples of 13 individuals on board a ship written by Earl David Wemyss (1494-1544):

> **October 30, 1518**: *"I begin to plan my trip to the Western Lands and have asked 12 of the brethren to travel with me."*
> **May 15, 1520**: *"We leave in the morrow for the Western Lands. Twelve of the brethren travel with me aboard the Elizabeth."*

We should also point out one more entry with two other sacred numbers found on the Kensington Rune Stone that are part of the Enochian legend of the Secret Vault allegorically embedded within the inscription which I named the "Cryptic Code". Those numbers are 10 and 14. This entry was written by John Weems immediately after the treasures left by Earl Henry and his men in Nova Scotia in 1395/1398, were recovered and brought to Mason's Island and placed inside an underground brick vault:

> **July 14, 1770**: *"A group of 10 and 14 masons encircled the tomb and we blessed the vault and asked Heavenly Father to bless and protect this place against time and the ravages and greed of war."*

Why this group of Freemasons and Patriots chose to divide the group up into 10 and 14 men, and not simply 24 men, must be related to the Enochian legend of the Secret Vault. For a group of men initiated in Masonic traditions they deeply honored those who were involved in such a secret and sacred mission, and literally standing above the secret vault they had just filled with treasures that would help bring the Covenant to completion, performing a ritual prayer to protect it would be expected.

Now let's turn to the Cremona Document. All these sacred numbers are based largely on the Fibonacci Sequence of whole numbers, 1, 2, 3, 5, 8, 13, 21... These numbers immediately jump out within a critical document found in the corpus of Cremona Document material; the Lionel de Waldern XXI's letter to Robert De LaSalle written on May 8, 1656. The sacred numbers begin with the date, May (5th Month) 8th,two numbers that were most likely intentionally selected, perhaps regardless of the date the letter was actually written. The sacred numbers continue within the body of the letter:

> I received a missive from Father Olier to go to his place of the Sulpicians to the north, above the large river. 26 (2 x 13) soldiers and Imogène and all the true-hearted people are also going to the north. I am sending 4 attached boxes with the 13 Adoniram's rolls, 26 (2 x 13) pharaoh's ones, 129 Euripid's ones, 9 (Enochian legend of the 9 arches and the Secret Vault) Cohan's ones, 16 (2 x 8) of ours, 8 Yeshua's ones and the Celt's story. I also sent the Lord's war book.

The most recent sets of documents Don acquired from Roberta included five encrypted messages, two of them that incorporated an inspirational phrase that also served as the cipher phrase in the longest of message once the anagram of twenty-four letters was figured out: "The Power of God is within you." This phrase appeared regularly in the 6,609-letter message. It was used to ensure the deciphered message was being decoded correctly. It appeared 13 times.

"The Power of God is within you" wasn't only thing that appeared 13 times within the longest message. Inserted as if to bless and protect the sacred information the letter "K" appeared 12 times with the final word in the message being the word "Kay." This made a total, yet again, of 13.

Lastly, Don and I both agree Map 8 might be the most important document of the vast amount of Cremona Document material. To us, it is no coincidence the basic structure of the layout of the map incorporates the two most prominent sacred numbers, it is the 8th map comprised of 13 parts. Both numbers are vital to the cosmology of Templar ideology and the veneration of the Goddess numerically expressed in the Fibonacci sequence. This numerical expression of the Templars sacred core beliefs provides a powerful argument for the veracity of both sets of documents.

THE GODDESS

Perhaps the most profound revelation of both the Cremona Document and the Sinclair/Wemyss Journals is the deep veneration of the Goddess by the leadership of the medieval Knights Templar and their ideological descendants, the Freemasons. She, and the symbolism related to Her, such as the sacred numbers of the Fibonacci sequence, were at the core of their beliefs, more especially the number thirteen. The number 13 is special because it is in the Fibonacci sequence and its association with the movements of the planet Venus. When viewed astronomically over 8 earth years, it creates a 5-pointed star. The ratio found within it is 1:1.618, which is the Fibonacci sequence, also called the Golden Ratio. When rounded to whole numbers, the Golden Ratio sequence is as follows: 1, 2, 3, 5, 8, 13, 21, etc. The number 13 comes into play with the number of Venus years during the same period of 8 earth years. The Fibonacci sequence is the key to life in the universe and ancient indigenous cultures and the Templars associated creation with the feminine, i.e., the Goddess.

The number 13 is also associated with the moon, another representation of the sacred feminine in the heavens. The moon has 13 lunar cycles of 28 days per year which coincides with women's menstrual cycles that average 28 days hence the feminine association. The writers of the journals invoked the name of the Goddess or the "Holy Mother" 39 times which curiously is 13 x 3. Here are a few examples:

> May 21, 1354 (8-year-old Henry Sinclair while in the Nova Scotia with his father): *Today we celebrated the Bright Mother Goddess Day with our new friends* [Indigenous people of Nova Scotia]. *They too celebrate the Great Goddess who brings life to them throughout the year. We have many similarities.*

> June 15, 1398 (A now 53-year-old Earl Henry Sinclair): *My men have made many friendships and the people have taught us much about their worship of the Great Goddess which is similar to the old religion of Orknades and Scotland. We share many common beliefs and Father Nicolas is making a record of their beliefs and rituals. Together we celebrated the initiation of his youngest son into manhood as he celebrates his 18th year.*

> June 24, 1432 (24-year-old William "The Builder" Sinclair while in Nova Scotia checking on the treasures and the knights left behind by his Grandfather Earl Henry): *We have traveled inland to the Big Stone Fort and have found a small group of 8 Knights who have long*

since completed the fort and now maintain their homes nearby. Each has married and although now elderly, they have taught their children well and they celebrate the rituals of Christianity as well as the rituals of the Great Goddess.

October 3, 1520 (26-year-old Earl David Wemyss upon his return from Nova Scotia): We have returned from the Western Lands without incident. The natives were friendly and helpful and took us to the sites to show that they have fulfilled their promise of protection to their and mine ancestors and the Great Goddess. We have shared stories, food, and smoke and return to Scotland knowing that all is safe and undisturbed."

June 9, 1665 (32-year-old James Wemyss while planting a second horde of Templar treasure at locations along the St. Lawrence River): We have found the next marker, more by accident than by design and see clearly that our destination will be extremely difficult to reach. The shadow of the marking stick shown by the star of the Great Goddess sends us in the southward direction.

June 29, 1769 (28-year-old John Weems in Abington, Pennsylvania, after checking on the treasures in Nova Scotia): The candle is dimming and about to go out. I must retire although I know I cannot sleep. Tomorrow I will begin my journey home with Brother Scott. I pray that the Holy Father and Holy Mother protect and direct me in this task. I also pray that my wife Kitty will understand another absence.

The Goddess is also featured prominently in the Cremona Document starting with the place where the ancient scrolls were hidden the Temple of the Goddess on Hunter Mountain in the Catskills of New York. This Temple is described in the *A Year We Remember* narrative, driving home just how central the Goddess was to the Templars and their ideological, and very likely, bloodline ancestors:

The ancient maps show a land of Onteora far to the west, but the route is far from certain. With the round disks we can read some of the ancient scrolls that reveal how the unclean fled to Tigwa and set sail for the kingdoms of Woton far to the north. To the place in the past where the Goddess commanded the outcasts of Solomon to erect a temple in her honor in the land of Onteora.

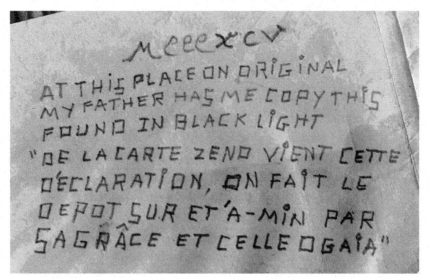

On the back side of Map 8 is a prayer in French that invokes the name of Antonio Zeno with a Hooked X, and a Hooked V incorporated into the Roman numeral date of 1395. "From the map of Zeno comes this declaration, we make the deposit on a-min by His grace and that of O-Gaia." (Courtesy of Donald Ruh)

The Goddess is also named in the French prayer on the back of Map 8 being called "O'Gaia", *Gaia* being the ancient Greek name for Mother Earth also spelled "Gaea," or "Ge" meaning Earth which is where our modern term "Geo" and the science of Geology comes from.[37]

It is important for the reader to understand that not only was the Great Goddess venerated by the Templars and the associated influential families, but they also had what they referred to as a Covenant with Her. A Covenant with ones' Deity is a sacred promise that must be fulfilled no matter how long or how many generations it takes, and in this case, it goes back to their first century bloodline ancestors who escaped the persecution of the Roman Catholic Church. They vowed to forever protect and keep carefully veiled the Great Goddess, who was demonized by the Church, along with women in general, who prior to the Roman occupation had always been considered equal to their consort, men. They asked that in return She would guide them on their quest to find a new sanctuary, a New Jerusalem, where they could worship Her freely and Her consort, Holy Father, in a Free State. The sanctity of the mission passed down through the Sinclair and Wemyss clans is appropriately summarized by John Wemyss with his entry on October 24, 1730:

---

37   https://www.etymonline.com/word/gaia

Before my father died last evening, he called me to his side and confided the secret of the Covenant between the Wemyss family and the Sinclair's of whom we are descended. Although I am his youngest son, he feels it is best to pass the responsibility to me as I am most likely to visit Nova Scotia as a member of the Kings army. My older brothers are loyal to the King more so than the Brethren and as the youngest I am able to travel more easily. I will remember his plea and have taken the journals to my possession. Although he has told me the story, he begs me to read the journals and take them me always to keep them safe and secret. I regret I cannot read the Old English, but my Latin is good, and I shall follow the instructions as best I can. My unit leaves next week for Jamaica, and I must make it my goal to achieve his last requests.

THE HOOKED X™

What might be the most powerful and sacred of all symbols to the Knights Templar and their ideological descendants the Freemasons, is the Hooked X. It is believed to represent Monotheistic Dualism, the belief in a single Deity with dualistic aspects of opposites that keep things in balance such as good/bad, light/dark, male/female, heaven and earth, and the Yin-Yang symbol. The Hooked X symbol appears 22 times on the Kensington Rune Stone, it is also found on four additional rune stones in North America that are believed to be connected to the medieval Knights Templar, the three Spirit Pond stones, and the Narragansett Rune Stone. Accordingly, it should come as no surprise to find many Hooked X symbols in both the Cremona Document and the Sinlcair/Wemyss Journals.

There are nine known examples of the Hooked X symbol in the Journals and thirty-five found in the compendium of the Cremona Document material. Bill Jackson recognized the importance of what he called, "...odd line on the upper r[igh]t quad[rant] of X." In 1973, he was told by Philip Roache, a man whose ancestors are believed to have had parts of the Cremona Document in the past, the symbol was a "cartographer's mark". Jackson then listed the names of members of the Poor Knights of Malta (Knights Templar) and they all turned up or were directly connected to the names on the back of Map 8

PHILIP ROACHE, WYOMING N.Y. 1973
POEM + CIPHERED MESSAGE BY GRANDDAD
BRASS NAIL ORIGINAL SOLD TO S.RHINEBARTD
ROACHE COPY QUELLE COATL, ANGRA PEQUENA
CIPHER KEYS USED BY J. P ROACHE, BLM'S MCDONALD
MACDONALS, F. BANNERMAN, DELORES.

ASKED ABOUT ODD LINE ON UPPER RT QUAP. OF X
AS (X) - PHILIP REPLIED. CARTOGRAPHER'S MARK

MEANS MEMBER OF POOR KNIGHTS OF MALTA AS A
NAVIGATOR OR CARTOGRAPHER
C. COLOMBO + H. SINCLAIR + VERRIZANO + P. DeLeon + R.De.
                                    SUPELEY

In this handwritten note by Bill Jackson in 1973 he relays being told the Hooked X symbol was a cartographer's mark used by navigators and cartographers who were member of the Poor Knights of Malta, another name for the Knights Templar. (Courtesy of Donald Ruh)

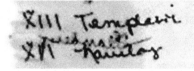

The Hooked X symbol is seen in the Roman numeral totals of the Templar Knights and seaman aboard the Accipiter, one of eight ships that traveled to the Western Lands under the command of Earl Henry Sinclair in 1395. (Wolter, 2016)

in Clyphus' historical narrative. Not coincidentally, there are three Hooked X symbols embedded within Roman numeral dates in the two blocks of text on the back side of Map 8.

LOGIC

The final point in the argument as to why the Cremona Document material, and the Sinclair/Wemyss journals by extension, are legitimate and important is the vast amount of material that has been vetted out. There are hundreds of pages of messages, sketches, and letters, and over two dozen maps. Most of the messages are encrypted in different ways including six "invisible" messages and maps that require extra steps to bring out the information. It's simply too vast and too complicated to be some kind of hoax or fraud. Further, there isn't an end game for a hoax or practical joke. Why would Bill Jackson drag Don Ruh to Newfoundland to scuba dive in the Atlantic Ocean and accidentally find a sunken twelfth-century ship? Why hike in the Adirondacks and the Catskill Mountains with Don searching for a temple and finding caves, carvings, and a tomb with remains and offerings, if it wasn't all based on legitimate historical information? Bill spent his own money for travel, research, and to purchase the document from the Benvenuto family in the first place. Twenty-three years later he sold the document for well over a quarter of a million dollars to an agent of the Roman Catholic Church. Clearly, they must have known what he had was legitimate to pay that kind of money. Based on what we now know about the sensitive nature of the material, it's obvious the Church would pay dearly to keep it suppressed.

It took many years for Don and me to finally realize how much material Bill had removed from the document and gave to his colleagues in the 1990s, knowing that someday these documents would end up with Don and finally be revealed to the world. That time is now and ready or not world, here it comes!

CONCLUSIONS AND
FINAL THOUGHTS

WHAT DOES THIS MEAN FOR *THE CURSE OF OAK ISLAND* SHOW?

Before weighing in on this question, Don and I must be honest about our negative bias toward the show based on our first-hand experiences. Don's negative feelings are certainly understandable, considering his unsettling experience with Zena—given they had a written agreement to write a book together based solely on the material that belonged to Don. Her decision to abandon Don, to bring the documents and artifacts he had loaned to her to the Lagina brothers was frankly, unforgiveable. It was a betrayal, plain and simple, for personal gain. While it is sad and unfortunate Zena passed away not long after she took the material to the brothers, it doesn't excuse what she did. To make matters worse, after her death, the remaining documents and artifacts Zena had borrowed from Don were given to the Lagina Brothers by her son. Don wrote a letter to the production company, Promethius Entertainment, the Lagina brothers, and the History Channel network asking for the return of the material. Don received no reply from any of them.

From our perspective this is unethical and frankly, disgusting behavior by all parties involved in the *Curse of Oak Island* show. This behavior leaves the impression that ratings and profits are more important than doing the right thing. After ten years of misleading their audience and chasing every rainbow their writers could create, the material Don received since Zena's fateful decision has proven the show has run its course. It is time to leave the island they pillaged for over a decade alone and let nature decide its future.

For my part, I find the treatment of Don by Zena and the *Curse of Oak Island* to be reprehensible. I remember the days leading up to Zena's decision to abandon Don and warned her not to do what she eventually did. Prior to this situation, I worked with Zena for several years and always found her to be kind, warm, and intelligent, but also very stubborn. Once she got an idea in her head it was difficult to get it out. The justification of her decision was partly based on events that occurred in Don's past that had to do with his work that were completely unrelated to their Cremona Document research, or their professional relationship. Frankly, I believes she was looking for any excuse to justify taking Don's material and presenting it as her own. Sadly, while that decision gave Zena a lot of attention in her final few years, it will stain her legacy forever.

Knights Templar

Don and I also believe the fact the treasures hidden in the "Underground Project" by the ideological descendants of the medieval order of the Knights Templar sheds important new light on the events that occurred in North America starting 600 years before the founding of the United States of America. Readers will likely be satisfied knowing the Oak Island mystery wasn't based on fanciful stories and beliefs and that what actually happened there was incredible and played an important role in what would eventually lead to the founding of the new Republic. It is also important to understand Oak Island was only one of several islands, and other locations, in North America where the Templars and their descendants' buried treasures and relics to be recovered in the future as part of the long-range plan they called the Covenant. The story is much bigger than Oak Island, but the mystery has kept this important story alive until it is now finally solved and put into proper historical context with the publication of this book.

The story of the founding of America began with the fugitive medieval Templars and was kept secret for six centuries but carried forward by brave and intelligent people who believed in the mission of establishing a sanctuary where people could live free from the tyranny of the monarchs of Europe, free from the persecution of the Roman Catholic Church, and suppression of the people when the Monarchy and the Church joined forces to oppress the people. This is why the founders insisted on freedom of religion and a form of government "by the people and for the people" that was ingrained in the Constitution. These tenants are especially important today when it seems the democratic principles within the Republic they formed are under attack. It's yet another historic example of how those who do not learn from the past are destined to repeat it. That is why the truth about what happened on Oak Island, and what happened elsewhere in North America after the put-down of the Knights Templar on October 13, 1307, is so vitally important today.

Money Pit

When it's all said and done, the answer to the Oak Island treasure mystery has been there since 1795. It was hanging from the old oak tree above the depression the young McGinnis boy found all those years ago. The only people who leave a block and tackle hanging from a tree above a depression in the ground are ones who didn't care about covering their tracks. Why it didn't occur to people for 229 years is surprising, but then, it's more fun to hold out hope for the mythical treasure to someday be found rather than accept the truth was there, way back then, hanging from the old oak tree...

ABOUT THE AUTHORS

Scott Wolter (1958-Present): Born in Homestead, Florida, Scott has worked as a Forensic Geologist running a materials forensic laboratory in St. Paul, Minnesota, since January of 1990. He hosted the cable television show, *America Unearthed*, for four seasons and forty-nine episodes. Scott has also appeared on several other television shows and streaming platforms such as *Pirate Treasure of the Knights Templar, Secrets of the Viking Stone*, and *Mysteries of the Knights Templar*, among others. Scott has written a total of ten books. Since meeting Don in 2006, Scott has worked on the Cremona Document material with him and many other researchers including Janet Wolter, David Brody, Steve St. Clair, Darwin Ohman, John Freeburg, Jerry Lutgen, Terry Tilton, and Hayley Ramsey.

Donald Ruh (1942-Present): Born and raised in Mount Vernon, New York, Don worked as an electronics technician until 1994 when he joined Lorad, making mammography equipment. He retired in 2008. Don is an honorary member of the New York State Archaeological Association and has been a member of the New England Antiquities Research Association (NEARA) since 1998, as well as a member of the American Audubon Society. Don was seven years old when he first met Bill Jackson, who was eleven years old at the time. They became lifelong friends and Don supported Bill for the twenty-three years he researched the Cremona Document until Bill sold it to Archbishop Paul Marcinkus in 1994. Because of this close friendship, Bill made sure the most important parts of the document he dispersed to colleagues with the agency they both worked for were left to Don upon their deaths. From 2017-2023 five of those colleagues have passed on, leaving Don with an incredible trove of Knights Templar historical material.